# The Compost Book

# The Compost Book

2nd Edition

## David Taylor
## Illustrations by Rob Allsop

**REED**
**NEW HOLLAND**

To the memory of Yvonne Taylor,
my partner & collaborator

# CONTENTS

# INTRODUCTION

Welcome to the world of waste and worms; to the magic of the microbes that convert muck into nutritious compost. Many wastes around us are useful and free, so gather up those grass clippings, tear up your newspapers, save your fruit and vegetable peelings, tea leaves, coffee grounds and even the contents of the vacuum-cleaner bag.

You are about to declare war on waste and want by composting just about everything. You will be amazed to witness the reduced volume of garbage and garden litter in your wheelie bins, as so much so-called rubbish can be recycled as compost.

Compost making works well as long as you understand its requirements. Basically it is a form of cooking; employing biochemical and microbiological reactions. A compost heap can be a sad mess, like a failed sponge cake. So read on, follow the recipes, add accelerators and understand the necessity of balancing ingredients. Both FAST and SLOW methods of compost-making are discussed. In this book you will find out what you can or cannot compost. Bins, boxes, tumblers, shredders and other composting tools are discussed and evaluated. You will learn about the various potencies of various animal manures and the useful properties of seaweed, a range of garden herbs and even weeds. Methods are outlined for making liquid manures and herbal teas, as well as using your compost in potting and seedling mixes.

You will also find the answers to questions you might have asked, such as:

- What's wrong with my compost? It stinks!
- What do I do about vermin in my heap?

- Is my compost ready?
- How do I use my compost?
- Is a worm farm the solution for my limited space—the unit balcony?
- I have a weekender, explain about composting toilets?

May this little book inspire you to action, leading to happy composting and more knowledge about improving your immediate environment by nurturing your soil through recycling so-called waste. Compost-making is an important aspect of garden preparation. RUDYARD KIPLING wrote there is more in gardening than meets the eye:

> *For where the old thick laurels grow, along the thin red wall,*
> *You find the tool- and potting-sheds that are the heart of all,*
> *The cold-frames and the hot-houses, the dung-pits and the tanks,*
> *The rollers, carts and drain-pipes, the barrows and the planks.*

# WHAT IS COMPOST?

Compost is a fundamental plant food emulating and assisting natural processes of enriching soil from which all your plants draw their nutrients. After a season of fruiting, flowering and vegetable production, your soil will be tired and need revitalising. It is important that your compost heap or bin is not treated as a dump for when you forget to put out the garbage bins on Sunday night. Composting is a biochemical process, a form of digestion, in fact. Like any digestive system it needs a balanced diet if it is to perform efficiently. A balanced diet is the key to a good compost.

Fig 1. Plant nutrient cycle

# Why Compost?

## Recycling

**Composting is a method for burying your carbon footprint.**
Composting dramatically reduces the volume of disposable waste.
I live too far out of town and I do not have a roadside garbage
collection. Thanks to composting I have very little rubbish to
consign to friends' bins in town. My garbage is reduced to flattened
cat-food tins, glass bottles, plastic wrappings, glossy magazines and
flyers. Most plastic containers are recycled as plant pots or food
containers. Tins with airtight lids store vegetable seed. Glass jars
are refilled with jams or chutneys.

Home-garden produced compost is more energy efficient than
consigning organic waste to land fill or commercial recycling. In
fact, our own physical efforts are the major energy inputs in
returning natural products to the soil, ultimately stimulating plant
growth. This return to source recycling by composting replicates
the continuum in nature as is shown in Figure 1: The Plant Nutrient
Cycle.

# More Productive Soil

The second reason is that composting converts decaying vegetation and animal waste into humus, which absorbs both moisture and nutrients in the lightweight, dark coloured material. When the humic-rich compost is incorporated within the soil, a more productive growing media, known as loam, results.

## SOIL + COMPOST = LOAM

Furthermore, the humus retains moisture by limiting evaporation, thus reducing the need to water frequently. Watering should always be at ground level, directly into the humus. I water through the black dribble hoses, of recycled rubber tyres, which wet the humic compost but does not turn the clay soil into mud. On drying, this clay tends to form a hard crust, inhibiting plant growth, so water absorption by the compost is critical.

Soil is the result of physical erosion and/or chemical corrosion reducing rock into fine particles. Although the fine mineral content may contain beneficial elements, the soil would be infertile but for microbial activity releasing essential nutrients from the rotting litter layer. The cycle in Figure 1 demonstrates that nutrients absorbed by plants from the soil eventually return to the soil as the litter layer decays. This decay of woody tissue is accelerated by bacteria, fungi, slugs and insects; particularly termites (white ants) in mainland Australia.

The rotting litter produces humus, which adds nutrients and retains moisture. In your garden, compost replicates the leaf litter accumulating in a rainforest. Humus turns soil into loam. The richer the loam, the greener the leaves, the brighter the flowers and the juicier the fruit. Increased plant strength assists resistance to pests and fungal attacks.

# YOUR SOIL TYPE AND COMPOST

Soil type varies from pure sand to pure clay with intermediary types depending on the proportion of various grain sizes. In the laboratory, sieving and weighing determines the soil type. For the home gardener, a visual estimate of type can be achieved by placing the soil in a jar, adding water and shaking. On settling there will be size sorting with the coarser sand at the bottom, grading up to silt and clay.

By adding rotted plant material or compost (humus) to the jar and shaking again, the plant matter will float on top. A drop in water level indicates that the humic compost has absorbed water and absorbed the fine clay particles that caused the clouding. This absorption clears the cloudy water column, further demonstrating the role compost plays in absorbing water and potential nutrients in the fine clay particles from the soil. If the addition of compost does not clear the water column, the plant material has not sufficiently decayed, as the outer resistant layers are shedding rather than absorbing the water, together with the suspended clay particles. Such compost needs further maturation by stimulating microbial activity by wetting and adding activators (refer to page 47). Soil with a very high sand content requires thoroughly matured compost, as unlike clay soils, composting will cease when added to sandy soil. Finally the third diagram in Figure 2 shows the structure and texture that is achieved.

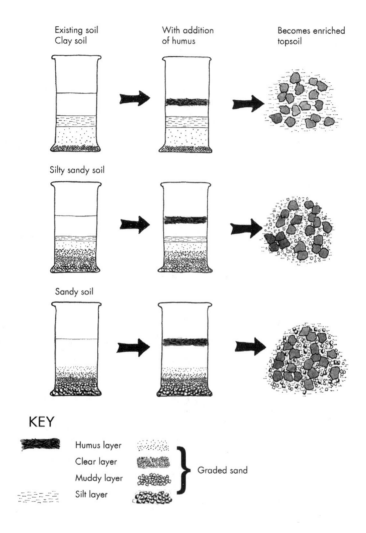

Existing soil
Clay soil

With addition
of humus

Becomes enriched
topsoil

Silty sandy soil

Sandy soil

KEY

Humus layer
Clear layer
Muddy layer
Silt layer

} Graded sand

Fig 2. Soil type soil plus humus equals loam

# Chelation

Mineral elements in the soil are congregated by bonding with organic compounds. The humus in the compost provides humic acids that drive this natural process, aided by earthworms and other organisms. This process is known as CHELATION (pronounced kee-lation) meaning claw-like, alluding to the attraction of humic acids to metallic elements.

Chelates are water soluble and stable, so they are readily converted into plant tissue. To observe the chelation process, remove moss or lichen from a weathered rock (especially granite). Beneath the moss the rock is fresh and shining compared with the worn surface of the rest of the outcrop. The claws of the chelating substances have extracted nutrient minerals, sustaining the moss in a soil-free situation. This mechanism permits lichen to grow in such hostile environments as ice-free rock surfaces in the Antarctic.

The drawings in Figure 3 represent spade-deep slices of my Redlands clay soil. Being wind-blown (Aeolian) in origin this clay contains a diversity of mineral elements, but was almost devoid of humus. Thus the aim was to develop the Redlands clay soil into a rich loam. In progression the spade-deep slices represent a developing topsoil from crusted clay surfaces. The effects of limited cultivation are shown, then with the regular addition of compost and animal manure, the soil profile is enhanced with the top soil expanding and deepening. The crusted soil has been chelated by the humic acids from the compost to develop a fertile top soil. This natural process is initiated by bacteria and fungi, then aided by various worms, insects and plant roots; even deep-rooted weeds.

Earthworms have a particular role in the incorporation of plant matter into a humic topsoil. There is a remarkable similarity between the right hand profile on Figure 3 and the soil profile 'of the vegetable mould in a field' as illustrated in Charles Darwin's book *Darwin on Humus and the Earthworm* (1945, figure 5). Darwin's field had long existed as poor pasture and was swampy. In 1835 the field was drained, spread with sand and within seven years had been reclaimed as productive pasture. Darwin attributes this reclamation to worm activity in the decomposition of vegetable matter into humus. Now we would consider this process as chelation, in which earthworms play a significant role. However, this does not diminish the pioneering observations made by Darwin, originally published in 1881.

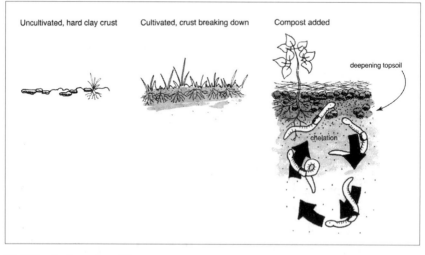

Fig 3. Developing soil profiles

# MAKING YOUR OWN COMPOST

If you live in the suburbs, making your own compost is dependent on space and availability of suitable materials. If space is available, a well constructed, covered heap is the simplest method, but this must be well away from neighbours. The heap should be layered with one part (volume) of kitchen waste and animal manure sandwiched between layers of three parts of fibrous materials, such as leaf litter, hay, shredded paper and sawdust. The heap should be covered with a plastic sheeting or organic carpet under-felt, but kept open at base to allow access to worms. Don't forget to keep moist

## Choosing a Site

Location of your composting area is dependent on space and proximity to neighbours. One of my friends in an inner-city suburb keeps her twin compost bins with the garbage bins in the car port. This seems a logical location as it involves only one trip to deposit compost, rubbish and recyclables. However, the compost bins are in the shade, whereas it is preferable to choose a sunny position to heat the compost.

Open compost heaps or stalls need to be well removed from your house and neighbouring residences.

A sunny position is desirable to accelerate the fermentation. An elongate, narrow windrow should be orientated east-west, to maximise solar heating. Lidded bins and boxes are not affected by rain, but open heaps and boxes should be covered with plastic sheeting to prevent a hiatus in the fermentation.

# Containers

Improvised bins and boxes can be constructed from timber, bricks or corrugated iron, as illustrated in Figure 4. A cylinder of wire netting provides aerobic conditions for decomposing leaf litter and pulled weeds as long as the filling is kept moist. A more elaborate construction consists of two stalls—one for accumulation, the other for maturation. The maturation stall can be fitted with a wire grid above ground, so that finished compost will fall through for collection.

A diversity of composting vessels is available. A survey of garden centres and hardware stores, as well as opinions by fellow gardeners, suggests that the more expensive, the more efficient the container. Most of these containers are basically maturation vessels and cannot cope with constant additions of moist material such as food scraps and fresh lawn clippings. A separate container is necessary so that this waste can be stock-piled before being mixed with fibrous carbohydrates when filling the composting vessel.

My preference is for a tumbler with the horizontal axle acting as a baffle to prevent clogging. The tumbler should be two-thirds full of suitable material at the start and turned daily. Periodic tumbling turns the bacterial community from an anaerobic to an aerobic mode. Friable compost should be ready within 14 days by following recipe for Fast 14 on page 40. Similar instructions apply for the rocker tumbler that rotates vertically, but the absence of a baffle may result in clogging restricting aeration and producing a smelly mess. The spiral compost tool could be used in this situation.

Lidded plastic bins open at the base allow entry by earthworms. Punch a few holes in the side for aeration and to prevent a smelly sludge developing. Having two bins is the ideal solution with one for stockpiling household waste and the other being progressively filled with alternate sludge and dry layers. However, the aerobin has a clever central column that allows air circulation, so that

Fig 4: Tossing and turning—bins, boxes, barrels

ingredients can be added continuously and finished compost removed from a door at the base with a tap allowing discharge of liquids. Although there is no need to stockpile kitchen waste, it is still necessary to mix with fibrous ingredients.

# Tools

Suitable composting tools are basic garden tools, such as a sharpened spade for cutting fibrous stalks and a garden fork for tossing or distributing compost piles. For larger heaps, a long-handled pitch or manure fork may be preferred. Recently a cork-screw like, spiral compost tool has appeared on the garden supplies market. As shown in Figure 5, this tool aerates and lifts material in a bin or rocker tumbler.

There is no need for a shredder or muncher. A sharpened spade is adequate unless your garden produces lots of prunings or tough plant stalks. Sometimes a machete or tomahawk is handy for chopping fleshy stalks, such as bananas palms. Some people spread out garden refuse and run over it with a motor mower, but it has never worked for me and I consider it dangerous as sticks fly in all directions.

Maybe you can share a shredder with other gardeners. If so, choose a petrol-driven model rather than the smaller electric ones that tend to clog. An office paper shredder is handy in making newspaper compost-ready, as well as bedding for worm farms, rabbits or guinea pigs. Check the capability of the machine before purchase.

Fig 5. Turning and aerating compost with the spiral compost tool

# COMPOSTING IN CONFINED SPACES

In restricted spaces, even unit balconies, worm farms are ideal for composting kitchen and other organic refuse. These farms, consisting of a stack of plastic trays, are available from garden centres, complete with instructions. Adequate food and bedding for the worms are essential. Kitchen scraps alone will result in a smelly glug and dead worms.

Worms gravitate into corrugated cardboard, so line the base of a tray with this or newspaper. Cover with a mixture of dry grass clippings and fallen leaves, withered weeds and, if available, hay or straw. On top of this bedding, add kitchen scraps, including tea leaves and coffee grounds, then scatter bran, cornmeal or seaweed meal on top. Cover with old towel or carpet under-felt and check moisture. The nutritious topping should be scattered each time more kitchen scraps are added. As the population multiplies, prepare another tray. This goes on top of the active tray so the worms can move 'up-market'.

For attracting garden worms, assemble the bedding and food layers in a box—wooden, plastic or even thick cardboard as long as spaces allow worms to enter from the bottom. Cover the box then keep it moist and in the shade. I use an old galvanised drum. (The toppings can be purchased from a bulk health food store.)

# KEY INGREDIENTS FOR COMPOST MAKING

The key ingredients for compost are tabulated at the back of this book, together with their uses and values. The principle ingredients are:

HOUSEHOLD WASTE including kitchen scrapes with peelings, tea leaves, coffee groungs, eggshells, as well as vacuum cleaner dust, fire ash and any other organic matter. This nitrogen-rich material is essential but should never be more than a fifth of the total content.

ANIMAL MANURES either fresh or dried. The specific attributes of the manure varies according to the source as outlined in Figure 16, but any manure is beneficial.

Pelletised poultry and cow manures are available commercially and they are convenient products being odourless and easy to handle. An important nitrogen source, together with other nitrogen-rich matter (e.g. kitchen scraps), they should never be more than 20% of total compost volume.

DYNAMIC LIFTER is a product incorporating poultry manure, from factory farms. It is a concentrated organic fertiliser, produced by composting methods, converting gaseous ammonia into soluble nitrate salts. It is useful if fresh manure is unavailable.

BLOOD & BONE a residue from meat processing has high phosphate values. Use as an additive.

WORM CASTES commercially produced from treatment plants are a fantastic phosphate rich organic fertiliser.

FILLERS WITH HIGH CARBON CONTENT should constitute 75% of volume of composting materials. These fillers include garden waste, grass clippings and dried leaves. If available, hay and straw are terrific fillers particularly if they have been used as bedding for hens, horses, rabbits or guinea pigs. Shredded newspaper and cardboard can be added to bulk up the compost, as can sawdust.

PEAT and COCONUT FIBRE have moisture-retaining qualities. Add to mature compost. It is particularly useful for seed trays, pot plants and balcony boxes. Test moisture by using the squeeze test (see Figure 7).

BROWN COAL from the Gippsland (Victoria) is being marketing in a pulverised form, under the trade name HUMATE. It would certainly be a moisture retainer (holding up to 20% dry weight) and may have chelating properties. Test moisture content by squeeze test.

LIMESTONE, DOLOMITE, GRANITE and BASALT help adjust the chemical balance. Although powdered, they are still an unaltered organic product. One cup to a compost bin is adequate.

SEAWEED in any form—fresh, dried, pulverised meal or liquid extracts— is a rich source of plant nutrients. With fresh seaweed, shred it and add no more than 25 per cent of total volume. With other seaweed products, read instructions. Fish based products such as CHARLIE CARP are also excellent additives, as long as you follow instructions.

HERBS fresh, dried or as a tea, especially borage, comfrey, stinging nettles, dandelions tansy and yarrow can be used. For recipes on herbal teas, see page 58.

# What Not to Include

The adage RUBBISH IN = RUBBISH OUT also applies for compost, illustrated by the cartoon in Figure 6. The following are either indigestible or undesirable in compost, so should be left out or treated with caution, as is the case for carpet under-felt.

TEA & COFFEE BAGS take years to disappear, but used leaves and grounds are good additives and ideal for worm farms.

CITRUS PEEL can cause acidity, which kills worms.

FRUIT STICKERS appear to be indestructible, so should be removed from peel, as they block up sieves and filters.

FRESH ANIMAL MANURE must be covered to stifle odours and swarms of flies.

HUMAN EXCRETA must also be covered to stifle odours and avoid flies, see also discussion on composting toilets (p.60–61).

DOG & CAT EXCRETA is undesirable for composting.

MEAT & FISH SCRAPS must be buried deep, otherwise it attracts cats or visiting vermin.

GLOSSY MAGAZINES break down very slowly and tend to cake with pages sticking together when wetted. Both glossies and newsprint are synthetics with no mineral based inks.

ANY PLASTICS including plastic-coated cardboard containers, such as wine casks (except for Banrock Station wine casks, which are environmentally friendly).

COAL FIRE ASH may be too high in sulphur. Ash and charcoal from Australian hardwoods are excellent additives.

SAWDUST FROM TREATED PINE is not recommended. Australian hardwood sawdust is fine for bulking up compost.

ARTIFICAL FERTILISERS including SUPERPHOSHATE, UREA etc. stimulate growth but inhibit soil organisms (Refer to p.62).

PREPARED ORGANIC FERTILISERS may contain synthetic nitrates so read the label.

CARPET & UNDERLAYS must be of totally organic fibre content, without plastic webs or backings. Even after heeding this warning, caution is necessary as some floor coverings may have been permeated with long-life insecticides. The presence of toxic substances can be checked by wetting a strip of carpet and laying it on the ground. If worms congregate under it within 14 days, it can be used to cover compost.

TINS and other METAL OBJECTS take eons to decompose. However, I have a stainless steel spoon pitted after 10 weeks in over-acidic compost.

Fig 6. Rubbish in = rubbish out

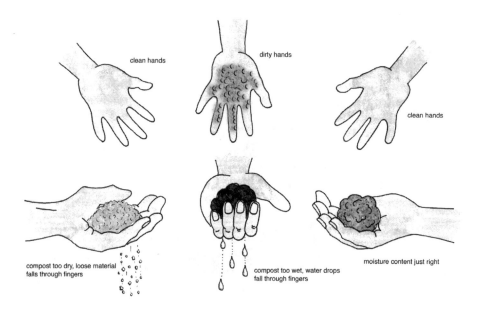

clean hands

dirty hands

clean hands

compost too dry, loose material
falls through fingers

compost too wet, water drops
fall through fingers

moisture content just right

Fig 7. Squeeze test for moisture content

# BALANCE

Compost needs 16 chemical elements for absorption by plant: 10 of them in small (trace) quantities, while the other six are major contributors. These six elements are oxygen (O) and hydrogen (H)—available from the atmosphere and from water—carbon, nitrogen, phosphorous and potassium, which have to be soluble for plants to absorb into their cells and tissues. Balance of the six elements is an important factor influencing plant growth. Maintaining a balance between carbon and nitrogen is fundamental and is the theme of the Compost Diet Cone (see page 30, Figure 8). More carbonaceous matter, such as hay, straw, paper and sawdust, is required than nitrogen-rich kitchen waste. For instance, one container of kitchen waste needs at least 10 containers of fibrous matter to achieve balance.

Balance of moisture and the alkalinity/acidity scale (pH) are not hard to achieve, but essential for the maintenance of microbes in the heap or bin. Your compost should be moist, but not sodden and smelly. The micro-organisms and worms will be decimated if the mix is too acidic or too alkaline. Two types of microbes are needed in your pile in order to convert waste material into compost: ANAEROBIC BACTERIA function within the heap or bin in airless conditions; AEROBIC BACTERIA need oxygen to be able to 'work-out' efficiently. Interaction between these two assemblages of bacteria provides the energy for the whole composting process.

The balance of ingredients is vital, particularly the CARBON/NITROGEN RATIO (C/N ratio). Ideally this ratio should be 25:1 by weight. If the carbon content is much higher, the heap will either stagnate or, if wetted, may spontaneously combust due to production of methane (as in hay stacks). Conversely, if nitrogen-rich matter, such as kitchen scraps and fresh grass clippings, dominate then a gluggy pile will develop.

# THE CARBON/NITROGEN
# COMPOST DIET CONE

All organic matter contains both carbon and nitrogen in varying proportions. The vital function of composting is to convert the carbon and nitrogen into plant food. The carbon content needs to be 25 times greater than the nitrogen content. Expressed another way, the C/N ratio should be 25:1 and never greater than 30:1.

If there is too much carbon, the production of carbon dioxide will be rapid and much of the material will have been consumed. The resultant compost will be greatly reduced in volume, light in colour and nutrient deficient. Too little carbon inhibits the production of biological energy in the pile, slowing the composting process. A dark smelly mess results.

To demonstrate the C/N ratio balance, imagine a three dimensional cone as in Figure 8. At the tip of the cone put in kitchen scraps, animal manure and lawn clippings. Fill this imaginary cone with dried grasses and leaves, shredded paper and sawdust. Cover and rotate the cone a number of times to thoroughly mix the ingredients. On maturation such a mixture would produce a well-rounded compost.

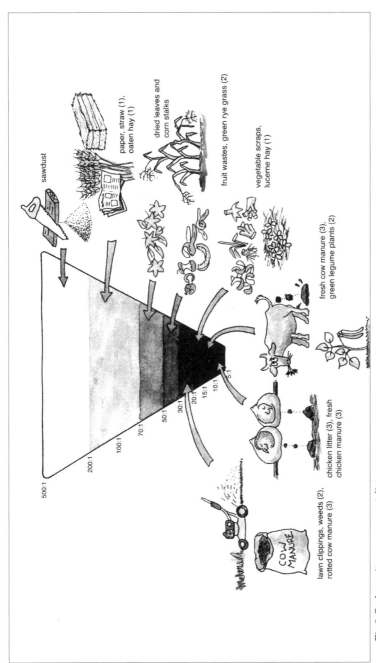

Fig 8. Carbon-nitrogen compost diet cone

sawdust

paper, straw (1), oaten hay (1)

dried leaves and corn stalks

fruit wastes, green rye grass (2)

vegetable scraps, lucerne hay (1)

fresh cow manure (3), green legume plants (2)

lawn clippings, weeds (2), rotted cow manure (3)

chicken litter (3), fresh chicken manure (3)

COW MANURE

500:1
200:1
100:1
70:1
50:1
30:1
20:1
15:1
10:1
5:1

# MOISTURE CONTENT

Balancing the moisture content of the compost heap is very important. If too wet, the compost will become a soggy mess. Bacteria cannot proliferate if the pile is too dry. Apply the 'squeeze test' as shown on page 28. If the compost is too dry, the material will fall through your fingers. If too moist, water will be squeezed out and your hand will be dirtied. If a discrete ball of compost results, then the moisture level is balanced.

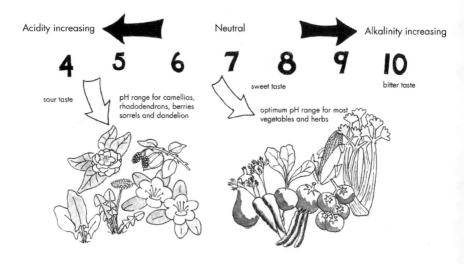

Fig 9. Acidity-alkalinity pH balance

# THE SOIL'S pH

Acidity/alkalinity balance is referred to as sweet or neutral if it is a value of 7 on the pH scale. See Figure 8. Below 7 acidity will sour the compost, gradually eliminating all biological activity. In the reverse direction, up the scale, alkalinity makes the compost bitter. Meters and pH test kits are available from garden centres and are reliable for testing the 'sweetness' of your compost.

Acid/Alkalinity levels can be adjusted by adding ground limestone or dolomite. It is debatable whether lime should be added during composting or spread directly onto soil.

Figure 9 illustrates that most vegetables and fruit prefer a pH ratio that straddles the neutral level of 7. However, a lot of berry fruit, including black and blue berries, prefer acid soil, as do sorrels and dandelions. If these plants flourish, their presence indicates acidity. Note: Figure 9 shows that the pH requirements for ornamental shrubs, such as azalea, camelia, gardenia and rhododendron, are not compatible with the pH requirements for most fruit and vegetables.

Carbon atoms are the cornerstones of all molecules within plants. They form carbohydrates and cellulose. In turn, these carbon compounds are converted into glucose to provide food and energy for growth. Oxygen is absorbed and combined with carbon to form biochemical compounds. On decomposition of plant material, carbon dioxide ($CO_2$) is generated by microbial activity as is diagrammatically implied in Figure 10. Under anaerobic, oxygen starved, moist conditions carbon atoms will combine with hydrogen to produce the inflammable gas methane ($CH_4$). Methane may cause spontaneous combustion; such as in stacked hay bales.

Yet production and reabsorbsion of these two gases ($CO_2$ & $CH_4$) is a prime function in the composting process and for making these three essential elements (C,O & H) available for plant nutrition. In fact this is a form of sequestration as the gases are removed from the atmosphere and stored in plants or well-constructed compost piles to mitigate the greenhouse effect.

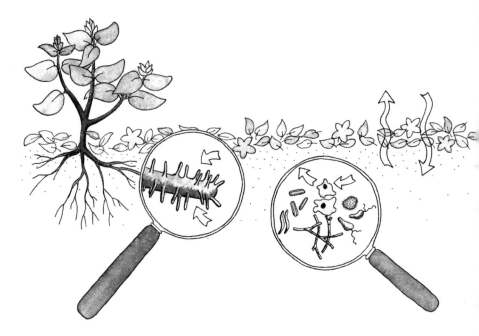

Fig 10. Oxygen-carbon exchange cycle

# THE NPK RATIO

The chemical symbols NPK signify the proportions of these three essential elements for plant growth; particularly food crops. NPK = 3:2:1 indicates 3 parts of available nitrogen to 2 parts of phosphorous to 1 of potassium. NPK ratios are shown on commercial fertiliser packets (both organic & artificial). The balance varies according to needs of specific plants. For instance, fruit trees need a high potassium content. NPK balance in your compost is a matter of trial and error.

Nitrogen comprises four-fifths of the air we breathe but it cannot be absorbed directly by plants. During electrical storms nitrogen can be bonded with oxygen and mixed with rainwater. The major source of nitrogen is from the microbial decomposing of organic material. Bacteria, moulds, fungi and other soil organisms release nitrogen fixed as gaseous oxides, ammonia or nitrate salts. The emission of ammonia from the soil will lead pigs or dogs to truffles and other fungi as illustrated in Figure 11. The Australian bandicoot uses a long nose for fungus finding.

Fig 11. Truffle hunting and nitrogen cycle

**Nitrogen** is a vital plant nutrient. It is the lynch pin in most biochemical molecules, including all protein, amino acid, chlorophyll and DNA molecules. Thus it is essential for leaf growth, seed fertility and genetic imprinting.

Until synthetic methods of fixing gaseous nitrogen were developed, the major source of nitrate fertilisers was Chile-saltpeter. The origin of these extensive deposits is problematic. Fresh animal excreta, especially from birds, have a high nitrogen content. Seaweed concentrates disolved nitrogen from sea water, making it a valuable source of nitrogen available for plants. As well as emitting ammonia, microorganisms fix nitrates within the soil in plant root nodules; particularly in legumes such as broad beans, peas, lucerne/alfalfa and clover.

**Phosphorous** (P) is the nutrient element for plant growth, putting energy into the biochemical systems. Involved in the production of chlorophyll and glucose, Phosphorus stimulates fruit development and the fertility of seed. Seaweed accumulates phosphates at a rate of 50,000 times greater than does seawater. All bird manures are richer in phosphorous than those from mammal manures. Pigeon manure has higher values than that from other domesticated birds (so find yourself a pigeon enthusiast!). Bones and other skeletal material such as prawn shells are rich in phosphorous. Other sources are guanos, which are accumulations of seabird or bat droppings. Earthworm casts also concentrate this vital element.

**Potassium** (K for Karium & Potash) is an important element in the biochemical process of forming starch, sugars and proteins, and in photosynthesis. Potassium is present in most organic matter. Wood ash is a slow-release source of potassium. Application of ash stimulates growth and fruiting of cucurbits (pumpkins, zucchini, melons etc) and is beneficial spread round the drip line of citrus trees. Unfortunately, with the demise of woodfires, ash is scarce in the suburbs. Synthetic potash salts are rapidly soluble, which may cause a chemical inbalance, inhibiting intake of other nutrients by plant tissues. Seaweed concentrates potassium; its content in seaweed is 140 times greater than it is in sea-water. Other sources of potash are soot and rock flours, particularly granite and basalt. So if your soil is granitic or basaltic you will not have a deficiency in Potassium.

All three of the NPK elements are essential for the process of photosynthesis. Photosynthesis is a complexity of reactions that convert solar energy into chemical energy in the presence of carbon dioxide and water for the manufacture of cell materials, as in green leaves, for plant growth. The carbon dioxide is generated by the decay of vegetation during the composting process.

Calcium (Ca) & Magnesium (Mg) are critical for vegetative growth, maturity and seed production. Although relatively abundant in the earth's crust, both elements are often deficient in sandy soil, such as those in the Sydney Basin. Such deficiencies can be rectified by spreading crushed rock dolomite, which has the dual action of adjusting the pH balance as well as the calcium/magnesium levels.

# Micro-nutrients

In minute quantities these trace elements are essential for plant growth and at the end of the food chain for human health. Boron (B), copper (Cu), chlorine (Cl), iodine(I), iron(Fe), manganese(Mn), molybdenum(Mo) and zinc(Zn) are the most prominent micro-nutrients often acting as catalysts rather than being incorporated within molecules. Deficiencies are reflected in plant growth abnormalities: for instance, whiptail in cauliflower is a molybdenum deficiency, while yellowing of citrus leaves indicates deficiencies in either iron or boron. Grain production and pasture growth improved significantly when a zinc deficiency was rectified in the south-east region of South Australia.

The presence of a trace element in the soil is a balance between being necessary due to a deficiency or becoming a contaminant. Zinc is an example of this paradox. High concentrations of any trace elements will be toxic to some plants and ultimately toxic to humans.

Each plant species has its own requirements and tolerances. Dramatic changes of vegetation cover revealed on aerial photographs or satellite images often indicate concentrations of a particular mineral containing a trace element toxic to the plant community, thus inhibiting growth. Such interpretations often lead to the discovery of vast mineral deposits.

Trace elements act as enzymes which stimulate organic function. Without enzymes plants could not grow, seed or reproduce; neither could they decompose. Without these enzymes, microbiological cycles could not operate and earthworm could not gather and concentrate nutrients in their casts. Compost, which includes a variety of materials such as legume hay, animal manures and sea-weed products, will contain a balanced mix of trace elements. Seaweed absorbs and concentrates micro-nutrients from sea water; magnifying iron content some 70,000 times, zinc by 15,000 and boron by 24. This is illustrated in Figure 12.

| Element | Concentration in seawater (mg/1) | Seaweed enrichment factor relative to seawater |
| --- | --- | --- |
| Carbon | 20.8 | x 12 300 |
| Nitrogen | 0.5 | x 8 000 |
| Phosphorus | 0.07 | x 50 000 |
| Potassium | 380.00 | x 140 |
| Calcium | 400.00 | x 750 |
| Magnesium | 1350.00 | x 4 |
| Sulphur | 885.00 | x 14 |
| Iron | 0.01 | x 70 000 |
| Manganese | 0.002 | x 26 500 |
| Zinc | 0.01 | x 15 000 |
| Boron | 4.60 | x 24 |
| Copper | 0.003 | x 2 300 |
| Molybdenum | 0.01 | x 45 |
| Iodine | 0.06 | x 500 to 25 000 |

Figure 12: The enriching properties of seaweed

# ASSEMBLING COMPOST

For maturation, it is best to add all components simultaneously rather than throwing in bits and pieces over an extended period. Stockpile kitchen scraps in a covered bin. If it is outside, the bin can be open at the base for hungry worms. Mix or layer this starter with other ingredients either as a covered heap or in a compost bin or tumbler.

## Fast Cooking-14 Day Compost

For establishing a new garden or revitalising an existing one, a quick fix compost can be created within 14 days by using this Fast 14 recipe. This method produces a reliable, nutritious mix. With careful preparation, it works every time without any special equipment, apart from a sharpened spade for chopping and a fork for tossing the mix. Quantities are given as per the filling of a 10-litre bucket. The product will cover about 4 square metres 10 cm thick. The quantities can be reduced but not increased, as larger quantities can inhibit fermentation. Also, larger heaps may make tossing difficult. The quantity stipulated will three-quarters fill a trumbler or rocker bin.

- 4 buckets fresh grass clippings
- 8 buckets garden waste chopped with a spade
- 1 small bale of legume hay or pea straw
- 2 buckets of bran
- 2–4 buckets of animal manure (depending on freshness and quality—say 2 of chicken but 4 from horse).
- 2 cups of molasses & ¼ cup seaweed liquid concentrate mixed in 2 buckets of warmed rainwater (can be purchased from garden & farm supply centres).

Mix ingredients well by tossing. Either pile on ground covered with plastic sheet or shovel into tumbler. Depending on air temperature, the pile will take 2 to 4 days to start cooking. Remember the thirsty bacteria don't function, so check moisture level. Your stock-piled kitchen waste can be added as a starter.

The graph opposite indicates that the mix should be tossed or turned every 3 days to aerate the pile. On aeration the temperature drops dramatically as the aerobic bacteria work out. These are replaced by the oxygen-starved anaerobic microbes which stimulate recurrent fever high temperatures. On cooling, a handful of dolomite and two handfuls of wood ash should be added. These additives stabilise pH and increase availability of the essential elements, potassium, calcium and magnesium. When the pile cools worms will move in. Note that the nutrient value of FAST 14 declines rapidly, yet maintains a well textured fibrous soil.

A spectacular demonstration of the heat generated by the Fast 14 composting process is to wrap fresh eggs in foil and bury them in the heating compost; say Day 3. Within 2 hours the eggs will be baked. Small potatoes wrapped in foil can also be Fast 14 baked.

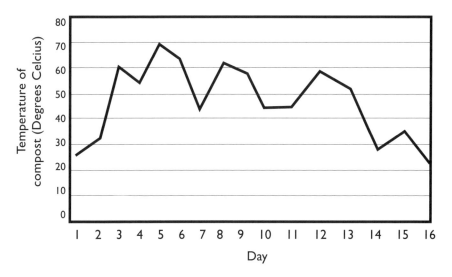

Figure 13: Fast 14 Compost

# Slow Cooked Compost

Well constructed layered heaps of compost (refer Figure 14) were proposed by Sir Albert Howard (Imperial Botanist in India-1905 to 1924). Howard developed his 'Indore compost-making process' scientifically for application throughout British India. Howard observed that the local Indians at his research station religiously returned all plant and animal matter to the soil. He proposed a link between healthy soil and healthy people. His Indore compost used only organic waste from local sources.

The method countered the spread of artificial fertilisers, which were imported and thus expensive. Furthermore, Howard, in his introduction to the revised edition of Charles Darwin's *The formation of vegetable mould* (Darwin, 1945), discussed examples that verified Darwin's observations, a century earlier, on the action of worms in creating and maintaining fertile topsoil. Furthermore, Howard cites evidence that artificial manures either reduce or eliminate altogether earthworm populations. Prolonged application of artificials resulted in reduced yields that were subsequently rectified by the age-old method of sheet composting, returning waste to the fields.

Meanwhile Rudolf Steiner, an Austrian philosopher, formulated the principles of bio-dynamic agriculture. Basically Steiner applied the same scientific principles as did Darwin and Howard, but he veiled them in meta-physics. As a result, bio-dynamics has been labelled unjustly as muck and magic. I can see science through the Steiner veil; particularly for the cow horn Preparation 500 and the ground quartz preparation 501. Biodynamic methods of compost making are described in detail by Wolf D. Storl in *Culture and Horticulture* (1979). Storl illustrates the application of herbal infusions of yarrow, dandelion, nettles, chamomile, valerian and oak bark, in homeopathic concentrations to construct a well constructed compost heap.

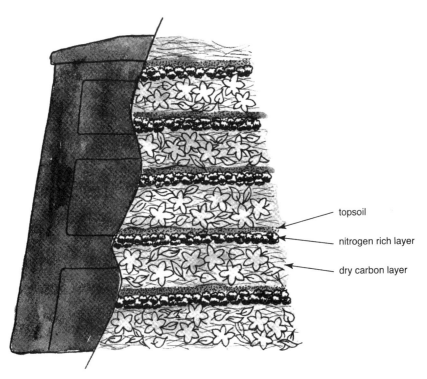

topsoil

nitrogen rich layer

dry carbon layer

Figure 14: A well-constructed Indore compost pile

At Glover's Community Garden (Rozelle, Sydney), just before Easter 1987, Rob Allsop (the illustrator) and I sliced up a pile of banana palm trunks and covered them with compostables and then soil. We then spiked this elongated heap with the herbal preparations in the order stipulated by Storl. By September the heap had subsided considerably. We probed the heap to discover that the banana trunks had totally decomposed. The resultant bed was sown and produced an abundance of cucumbers, followed by a good yield of potatoes and finally some long, sweet parsnips. As a compost it was the best I've ever made, but I still don't understand why. The herbal tinctures contain a powerful array of biochemical compounds; especially yarrow and valerian.

Whether it be Howard's 'elongate windrows', Darwin's worm farming or Steiner spiking the compost with various bio-dynamic preparations, decomposition can take up to 14 months. However, all available nutrient elements will have been incorporated. In summary, Fast 14 is available quickly to start a garden, whilst the Slow 14 is mellowing for a long life of nurturing the soil.

# MY SLOW 14-MONTH COMPOST

As I have the luxury of space with no immediate neighbours I accumulate my compost in a windrow (see figure 15), an elongate hump orientated east-west to fully utilise solar heating. It is never more than 2m wide. My windrow is forever changing, with fresh material being added at one end whilst finished compost is taken from the other end. The middle is occupied by a flourish of pumpkins in summer and autumn. In winter and early spring the windrow is aerated and mixed using a pitchfork. Longer windrows can be aerated by mechanical means. The ingredients are predominantly plant refuge, including weeds before they have seeded. Any thick stalks are munched or chopped with a spade. Chicken litter, sawdust, wood-fire ash, the dried toilet compost, contents of the vaccum cleaner bag and my stock-piled kitchen waste are dug in when available. Worms congregate in rich pockets of kitchen waste and the toilet compost, with the 'rocking horse manure'. A dribble hose keeps the heap moist, especially when pumpkins are developing.

Figure 15: Slow 14 windrow composting

It is possible to speed up slow 14 composts with organic accelerants. Adding fresh manures and fresh lawn clippings will have an instantaneous effect. Combining them with bran, fresh seaweed, liquid seaweed concentrate, yeast of any kind, yoghurt and/or molasses will prolong fermentation. Being long chains of glucose molecules, molasses fuels the fermentation process.

Commercial compost activators are available and from their listed ingredients they are no doubt effective, but you can make your own at a fraction of the price.

Make a hole in the pile and fill it with 5 parts fresh grass clippings and one part fresh horse manure. Sprinkle bran on top. Add 40ml of seaweed concentrate, 250ml of molasses and 250ml of yoghurt to 10 litres of warmed rain water. Mix well and pour mixture into the hole. Cover with more compost material. Note that this activator is in the formula for Fast 14.

# ADDITIVES AND ACTIVATORS

As mineral nutrients are incorporated within the organic molecules, decomposition releases these nutrients to be readily absorbed by growing plants. For instance, stinging nettles and dandelions are rich in iron—vital in the synthesis of chlorophyll, while comfrey, borage and tansy leaves are rich sources of potassium, phosphate and calcium.

Chamomile leaves and flowers not only add calcium but subdue odours emitting from your compost. Garden sorrel has a high copper content. Probably the most intriguing plant is yarrow, a member of the genus *Achillea* which was mythologically significant in the legend of Achilles' heel. Biochemically, yarrow is a powerful compost activator as it contains a complexity of stimulants for microbiological activity. Yarrow makes a very potent liquid tea, which is used in one of the biodynamic compost preparations.

Seaweed in any form is a wonderful compost activator and nutrient source. 'Rocking Horse Manure' (p.X) slowly releases essential elements, assisting in fruit formation; particularly citrus and pumpkins.

Some rocks crushed to a powder are excellent mineral additives. Most igneous rocks formed under extremes of temperature and/ or pressure contain high potassium and calcium values as well as traces of micronutrients. Igneous rocks such as granites and basalts provide key elements to the compost and texture to porous sandy soils, acting as clays. A monumental mason may supply you with this valuable dust.

Lime is applied to reduce soil acidity. Also, liming introduces mineral nutrients and conditions the soil by preventing water-logging. Crushed limestone (calcium carbonate) or dolomite (calcium & magnesium carbonates) are liming agents. The weak organic acids release carbon dioxide from the rock flour leaving in the soil alkaline hydroxides of calcium and magnesium to be absorbed by the plants.

To succinctly express this reaction:

$$CaCO_3 + MgCO_3 + HUMIC\ ACIDS$$
$$=$$
$$CO_2 + Ca(OH)_2 + Mg(OH)_2$$

As most limestones and dolomites are deposited in seawater they may contain traces of other minerals. The use of dolomite is beneficial in many Australian soils, which are deficient in magnesium; especially the sandy soils of the Sydney Basin. Dolomite should be available at your garden centre, otherwise you can order it in.

The source of the essential element phosphate is led by supply and demand. The battlefields of the Napoleonic wars were stripped of skeletal remains. These were burnt to release phosphates for the grain fields of the British Isles. When this supply was exhausted, bat guano deposits were excavated from caves, worldwide. Equatorial oceanic islands were then discovered to be thick piles of bird droppings on porous coralline limestone. Islands like Nauru and Ocean were denuded of this rich guano. Today our phosphates come from north and west Africa. Some phosphate rock is mined in north-west Queensland.

Phosphate rock is barely soluble in water, but in a powdered form, humic acids in the soil will release phosphorous. The oceanic island deposits from sea birds contain an array of mirco-nutrients with the essential elements. In the form of reactive rock phosphate (RPR), it is a terrific compost supplement; having been heat treated to increase solubility, so is readily absorbable by plants.

Gifts from the sea are nutritious enhancers as seawater contains all elements essential for plant growth. Some people even add diluted seawater to compost; say one part of seawater to one hundred parts of rain water. Asparagus, kale, New Zealand spinach, beetroot, silver beet and pig face all originated from coastal fringes, thus can benefit from application of dilute seawater.

Seaweeds further concentrate the nutritious elements from seawater. As as already listed, the NPK values for seaweed are prestigious. Furthermore, trace element values are elevated because the complete range of necessary trace elements available in seaweeds at values elevated from those in seawater; especially for iodine, a vital enzyme for human hormonal function (refer to Figure 11). Thus in any form, seaweed is an excellent compost ingredient. If collecting stranded seaweed from a beach check first with the local authority. Don't take growing seaweed. Once collected, hose off any evaporated salt, chop with a spade and cover in your heap or immmerse in a container of water. This tea can either be sprayed directly onto plants or added to the compost.

Nutra-Kelp, a concentrate fermented from fresh bull kelp, is recommended. It may seem expensive but 10ml in a 1000ml of rainwater is an effective spray for most plants. Add 20 to 40ml to your kitchen scraps. Be aware that some seaweed liquids are not fermented but extracted from dried material with synthetic nitrates added. Fish emulsions, such as Charlie Carp, are reliable products. They are odourless and use undesirable fish; such as the European Carp in the Murray Basin. The value of fish in the soil was understood long ago. The ancient Incas, in South America, plant corn seed into a hole on top of a sardine head.

Dried seaweed as well as seaweed and fish meals are useful sources of the full range of plant nutrients but are less powerful yet more expensive than the fermented liquids. All these products are available from garden supply centres, though you may have to hunt for specific brands or use the internet. Remember, the larger the container, the cheaper the unit quantity.

# COMPOST'S LITTLE HELPERS

So far the emphasis has been on the role played by simple microorganisms either in or on the soil; protozoa bacteria, fungi, lichens, mosses, moulds and yeasts. Simplistic in cell structure, yet complex in their environmental interactions, their life and work creates and maintains soil in a way that sustains plants. Temperature, moisture, aeration and pH dictate micro-biological activity. Given the right conditions for a particular group of organisms, its population will develop explosively. For example, when the compost is tossed and aired, the anaerobic bacteria that flourish in a closed heap will be almost instantaneously replaced by an aerobic population. Microbes form an impressive microcosm—within a gram of soil the population estimates can be astronomical with:

100,000 algal cells

1,000,000 fungal cells

1,000,000,000 bacteria

A legion of invertebrate animals play a significant part in the decomposition and redistribution of organic matter. These include various worms, slugs and snails, slaters, beetles, termites and a vast range of other insects.

The dung beetle is an outstanding example of a natural recycling system. This scarab beetle rolls up balls of cow dung, burying them to provide food for germinating eggs. Burying the dung not only reduces the fly population in the paddock but fertilises the paddock at the same time (See Figure 16, adapted from Heath, 1989).

'Nature's ploughshares' was Charles Darwin's pithy summation of the earthworm creating and maintaining topsoil. Darwin wrote that 'it may be doubted whether there are any other animals which have played such an important part in the history of the world.' He concluded that all humus in English soil had passed and will pass, time and time, again through the intestinal tracts of earthworms.

The mucus lining of the earthworms' guts and their burrows harbour bacteria that break down leaf litter in eco-systems. In a temperate grassland with a complex earthworm community, burrows contain a higher percentage of nitrogen fixing bacteria, both aerobic and anaerobic, than in the surrounding soil. Similarly, worm casts contain higher concentrations of essential elements than in the surrounding soil and vegetation. For these reasons earthworms enhance the nutrient content of your garden loam. So your soil should be regularly fed with humic material, which in turn feeds the earthworms. Worm casts are probably the richest organic source of plant nutrient.

Earthworms can be farmed in the confined space of your courtyard or unit balcony as an alternate method for composting kitchen waste. Commercial worm farms are readily available and a

Figure 16: The eco-friendly dung beetle

'wriggle of worms' can be purchased. Where more space is available the earthworms will find their way into open bins, active compost heaps and finished piles. Worms follow the food, migrating from finished compost to fresh kitchen waste.

Earthworms are very reliable environmental indicators as they cannot tolerate toxic conditions caused by contaminants or inbalance of pH. I have already suggested observing the presence or absence of earthworms as an indicator in using carpet under-felt, fresh animal manures and certain fruit peelings in your compost pile or worm farm.

# Even Pests Are Helpers

Although much loathed for their destructive activities in the garden, slugs and snails do have a function in the composting process. Their rows of teeth, called radulae, and their mucous membranes digest cellulose, including newspapers and cardboard. The most efficient is the large spotted leopard slug, especially as it eats only dead vegetation, newspaper and cardboard. Leopard slugs devour mould on wet surfaces such as the grout between tiles in your shower recess.

Slaters are cursed unjustly. Also known as wood lice or pill bugs, these land-living crustaceans have an active role in the decomposition process, grazing on yeasts, moulds and fungi. Slaters within a compost heap indicate that moisture levels are just right.

# ANIMAL MANURES

Animals compost plant material in their digestive systems. So the attributes of various manures are dictated by the physiology of their systems.

'As scarce as rocking horse manure' is an age-old expression. It need not be scarce, as you can create your own nitrogen-rich additive: Loosely fill a plastic container with sawdust add urine, cover and leave until liquids are absorbed by the saw dust to become a slow release organic fertilizer. Wood charcoal can be added to boost potassium content and to absorb and thus retain ammonia for subsequent release. In hot weather the mixture may ferment. Incorporate into your heap, bin or tumbler. Do not apply directly onto plants, though it is beneficial when sprayed on the ground around the drip line of citrus trees.

ELEPHANT MANURE is greatly overrated. There is an urban myth about the vitality transmitted to plants by elephant manure. Circuses are followed to collect the droppings. Though high in fibre, nutrient values are no higher than horse manure, but it has one advantage; the size and cohesion of the pats make them easy to collect. Some zoological gardens package ZOO POOH as a fundraiser, but the mixed sources of the product suggest that the quality as a fertiliser varies considerably.

PIG MANURE is rich in potash. When well matured, it will stimulate root and tuber growth, especially leeks, potatoes, sweet potatoes and yams. Maybe it's significant that pigs dig for food, including fungi, in the wild.

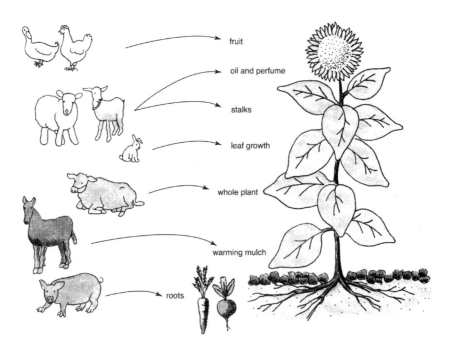

fruit

oil and perfume

stalks

leaf growth

whole plant

warming mulch

roots

Fig 17. Attributes of various animal manures

HORSE MANURE is fibre-rich, nutrient-low and was described by an old dairy farmer as 'all piss and straw'. Horses are not ruminants, like cows and sheep, so feed passes through them fairly rapidly, resulting in sloppy dung. In spite of this, horse manure, high in ammonia emissions, makes excellent composting material or can be used as an insulating mulch. When fresh, it heats quickly so is used as hot beds for raising seedlings in early spring. Matured, it is an excellent water-retaining mulch and a binder in unconsolidated soil. The binding property is apparent when added to clay in brick making.

As stabled horses are given high protein food, stable manure is believed to be high in nutrients. However, if the stables were sprayed with insecticides or the horses dosed with antibiotics, the manure could have retained these toxic substances.

COWS are ruminants and thus efficient digesters of vegetation, especially fibrous grasses and hay. Their composting vessel is known as a rumen. See Figure 18 for a diagram. Here food is transmuted by a myriad of bacteria and other micro-organisms. Cellulose is reduced by enzymal action to a pulp and regurgitated for further chewing. It then passes through the true stomach for final digestion. This highly adapted cellulose splitting system, takes eighteen days to complete.

The cow's stomach is oxygen-starved, so the microbial assemblage is anaerobic. But once eliminated onto the paddock, oxygen changes the assemblage to a dynamic aerobic one, releasing an array of nutrients, enzymes and microorganisms. Fresh cow manure is very beneficial in starting and enriching the composting process. Matured dung is terrific worm food. Basically, cow manure is a stimulant for strong plant growth.

SHEEP AND GOATS, like cows, are also ruminants, but the manure differs considerably. Sheep and goats drop dehydrated pellets with a relatively high potash content. This dung also contains a range of biochemical compounds which increases the aroma of fruit and flower as well as the oil content of Mediterranean herbs and olives. When sheep or goats graze on mint the oil content of the mint is concentrated. (Perhaps this is why we serve mint sauce with roast lamb!)

The accumulation of sheep manure under shearing sheds becomes a problem to the farmer, yet to me it's a gold mine and city gardeners bless you for a gift of sheep manure. Add to finished compost or spread generously over spoilt hay on established beds. Outstanding results can be achieved; such as sweet peas with bright colours, intense perfume and thick flower stalks up to 30cm long. This reflects the high potassium levels reinforcing stalk, stem and root fibres.

RABBIT AND GUINEA PIG DROPPINGS are very acceptable compost additives, especially with bedding litter of fine hay or shredded newspaper. These manures are rich in nitrogen, so stimulate leaf growth. If kept in a suburban backyard, follow advice regarding backyard hens given below.

POULTRY and OTHER BIRDS have only one elimination tract, the cloaca. Solids and liquids are vented together (See Figure 18). Thus poultry and other bird manures are rich in urea, the prime nitrogen source. All bird manures have high phosphate values; magnified in duck, pigeon and sea bird droppings. Bird manures, with their elevated phosphate value, enhance fruit formation and ripening.

Do not apply fresh poultry manure directly. Let it mature in a covered heap. When worms invade the heap, it is ready for the compost. If spreading directly onto prepared beds, mix into rotted hay, sawdust or shredded paper. Better still is 'chicken litter' that is pre-mixed. Another method is to make 'chicken tea' or use in the strip trench system (Figure 23).

The domestic hen is a efficient producer of compost when housed on deep litter, fed on spare vegetable leaves, selected kitchen waste and mixed grain. The litter of hay or straw is turned continually by the birds. Large hens contribute some 10kg of manure per bird per year and don't forget the eggs! For suburban yards, bustling little bantams or Chinese silky fowls are ideal and make charming pets. If the chooks are properly housed with deep litter and all uneaten kitchen scraps removed, there will be almost no smells or flies. Maybe you can let them free range from their house. Contact your local authority regarding regulations for keeping hens. Roosters are not welcomed, especially at 3am!

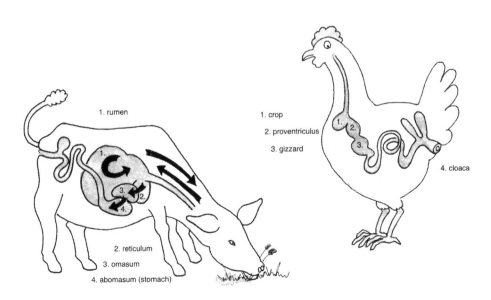

Figure 18. The cow and chicken digestive systems

# Herbal Teas And Liquid Manures

Herbal teas and liquid animal manure are a convenient form of composting in a limited space. Comfrey, stinging nettles, dandelions, parsley, yarrow, tansy and even cabbage leaves make beneficial teas with concentrations of various essential nutrient elements and biochemical plant stimulants. To make a herbal tea, lay the herbs, leaves, stems and/or roots in a container. Fill with rainwater and cover with a fitting lid. Stir every day or so. After three weeks it should be coloured green/brown and ready for use.

It is difficult to be precise regarding quantities for the mixture, as it all depends on how much is available. The container should be loosely filled with herbs, which can be a mixture of a number of species; say comfrey with dandelion and yarrow. Now cover with water. Decant and pour directly into your compost. For direct spraying, dilute to reduce the colour intensity.

Animal manures are best placed in a hessian (burlap) sack or thick perforated plastic potato bag, suspended in a covered container of rainwater, as illustrated in Figure 19. After 3 to 4 weeks the liquid can be drawn off and more rainwater added. This is a very economical method of applying cow or sheep manure, as refilling can be repeated 2 or 3 times, then the bag can be emptied into the compost heap.

When any odours have subsided, herbal teas and liquid manures are diluted and sprayed directly onto the plant or watered in around the roots. Undiluted they can be poured directly into the compost. Liquid chicken manure, with high nitrates, is a rapid compost accelerator. For a slow release fertiliser, soak charcoal in your liquid concoctions, then fork it into the compost. Fresh seaweed can be treated in a similar manner, after it has been hosed to remove any

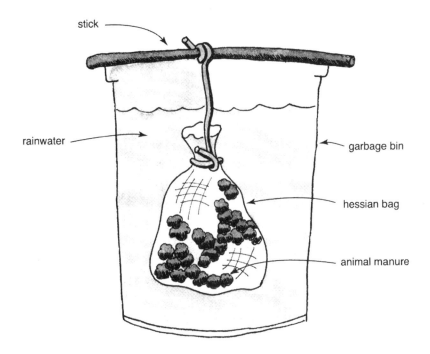

Figure 19. Producing liquid animal manures

salt. I add animal liquid manures directly to the compost and never spray directly onto plants. The seaweed liquid can be diluted until the colour and odour is almost neutral.

# Human Waste

A biocycle system for grey water is applicable if your wastes feed into a septic tank. The overflow spills into an inground holding tank until it activates a submersible pump which circulates this liquid compost around the orchard (see Figure 20).

My system is easy to maintain and automatically nurtures the heritage apple trees. Inquire regarding local regulations. There are more sophisticated systems that feed the waste water through mini-wetlands in order to purify the water, rather than merely distribute it as liquid compost.

## Composting Toilets

These range from the simple, with forced air circulating, to complicated solar-operated ones. Mine is a nature-loo 'compact' composting toilet, simple but adequate for one or two adults. The Nature-Loo, conveniently housed in the old garden 'dunny', has operated for 12 years without any problems. It has two chambers, one active, the other disconnected to mature. Air is circulated in the active chamber by a 12 volt exhaust fan. The chamber is divided by a grid so that fluids run off through a hose at the base (refer to Figure 20). The dried, matured compost is easily emptied and covered in the compost pile where it is rapidly devoured by earthworms.

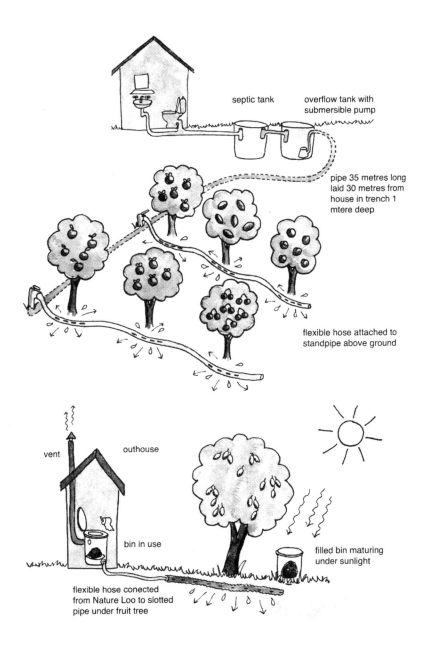

Figure 20. Bio-cycle and Nature Loo composting systems

# Artifical fertilisers versus organic methods:

Artificial fertilisers are synthesised by chemical manipulation so that they are soluble for absorbsion into plant tissue.

Superphosphate, commonly referred to as 'super', is manufactured by treating rock phosphate with sulphuric acid. Phosphoric acid, a more soluble form of phosphate, is released. 'Super' contains an abundance of sulphate salts increasing acidity that cause microbiological inbalance and are deleterious to earthworms. 'Super' inhibits the recycling of nutrients and does not enrich the soil, post harvest. 'Super' impairs the quality and nutritional value of some food crop. Compare Biodynamic (BD) rolled oats with those in packets from the supermarket. The BD oats feel oily and creamy when cooked. The packet oats feel and cook dry.

The great break-though in chemical based agriculture was the fixation of atmospheric nitrogen into highly soluble nitrogenous compounds. These compounds stimulate growth with prestigious chlorophyll production, yet no nutrients remain in the soil, which has to be top-dressed with nitrates or urea before the next crop. These days you need a permit to purchase quantities of these nitrogenous fertilisers as they are a principle ingredient in improvised explosive devices (IEDs). Exploding lettuces? Yes, being force fed, green vegetables do explode figuratively; often with unnaturally vivid green outer leaves (see cartoon in figure 21). Supermarket lettuces taste watery, whilst homegrown or farmer market produce have an earthy taste that reflects the nutrient mineral content.

Sir Albert Howard (1945) fully appreciated the detrimental effects of use of artificial fertilisers on the health of the soil and soil organisms and ultimately on our health. He also saw the economic consequences of acquiring transported artificials by

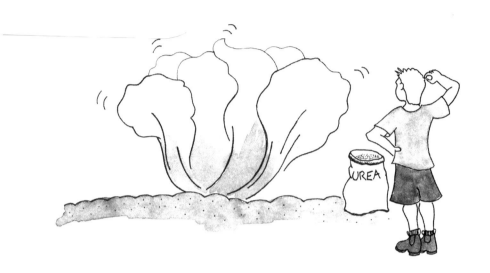

Figure 21: Synthetic nitrates and the exploding lettuce

Indian villagers. Manufacturing and transporting superphosphate and synthetic nitrates are high-energy consuming industries. Compared to chemical agriculture, organic methods are environmentally friendly, with minimal energy input. Composts and animal manures improve long-term fertility and texture in soil by sequestrating carbon dioxide, methane and ammonia.

# Frequently Asked Questions

## Why Does My Compost Stink?

The carbon/nitrogen ratio is out of balance, due to an overload with kitchen scraps and fresh lawn clippings. Your compost needs an immediate input of cellulose, as in straw, shredded newspaper, sawdust and dried leaves. Mix well, using the corkscrew compost tool or tossing with a pitchfork, making sure that the heap or bin is properly drained. Check moisture level by squeezing a sample in the palm of your hand as demonstrated in Figure 7 (page 28). If there are maggots in the soggy compost, sprinkle on lime, dolomite or fire ash to kill them.

## Why Is My Compost Is Riddled With Vermin?

The cartoon in Figure 22 contains the answer to this problem. The fermentation process is delayed and the heap is stagnating, due to inbalance in the carbon/nitrogen ratio and is moisture deficent. To elevate the temperature, use activators (See recipe p.46). Check moisture using the squeeze test. Moisten the thirsty microbes and cover. The vermin will vacate the heap or bin. Ants in the compost either shows it is too dry or that the compost is finished.

## Is My Compost Ready?

Take its temperature to see if it's cooled as shown on the temperature graph in figure 13. Is it friable with almost total decomposition? If you can pick out fragments of eggshells or chopped cabbage leaves or stalks, wait a little longer. It is not ready if it smells or dirties your hand in the squeeze test. The ultimate indicator is the presence of earthworms. They will occupy the heap when the temperature is equitable, the pH is neutral, the moisture content is balanced and no toxic substances are present.

# How Do I Use My Compost?

If the compost is on the ground, toss with a pitchfork, after adding a cup or more of lime or dolomite; depending on volume and whether it has been limed already. Empty friable material from bins or tumbler/rockers and add dolomite as required. Well-matured cow and sheep manure can be incorporated at this stage. Spread 5cm layer on prepared beds and lightly fork into topsoil, aerating at the same time.

TRENCH COMPOSTING SYSTEM:

If the volume of compost is not enough to cover the bed, concentrate the available humus by strip trenching (see Figure 23). With a narrow hoe, dig trenches 10cm wide and 10cm deep, spacing them 10cm apart. Fill the first and third trench with fresh animal manure and any chopped fresh organic matter; fill the middle trench with matured compost. Sow seed or transplant seedlings into the middle compost trench. Worms will be attracted to the maturing compost in the outside trenches. Once the first planting has been harvested, sow into the outside trenches, which now contain matured compost. Finally, fork over to amalgamate loam from all three trenches.

Figure 22: Too hot and moist now for vermin

The favourable rotation sequence is leaf vegetables, followed by root crops and finally legumes (eg. broad beans, peas).

## THE ESTHER DEANS METHOD:
## GROWING WITHOUT DIGGING

First published in 1977, Esther Deans' *Gardening Book* explains Esther's unique no-dig gardening system. Box in a small area with wooden planks, sleepers or bricks. A thick layer (say 5mm) of newspaper is placed on the ground; even on a growing patch of lawn. The paper acts as a weed mat. 'Biscuits' of lucerne hay are then laid to provide a nitrogenous source with organic fertiliser sprinkled on top. Cover with about 20cm of loose straw. Then finish with a circle or strips of compost, 10cm thick. The garden bed composts down and the layers melt into each other.

## RAISED BEDS:

Figure 23 illustrates our adaption of Esther's method by raising the beds to 60cm; the standard width of a sheet of recycled corrugated iron. On top of the paper we shovelled in clay mixed with a little sand, gravel and concrete rubble to aid drainage. The level was then raised to 30cm, with good loam mixed with pig or sheep manure. 'Biscuits' of pea straw were sprinkled with dolomite and fire ash. The beds were finished to 50cm with matured compost. Within 18 months the layers have blended by chelation with the top soil expanding into the clay sub soil.

Rather than planks, sleepers or bricks, we prefer to use corrugated iron as it presents an obstacle for snail and slugs and lacks nooks and crannies where they can hide. The rectangular beds can be any length, but the width should be twice the single arm span of the smallest gardener, so everyone can weed in the middle! We also filled 60cm high rings from old water tanks. Prefabricated galvanised frames, both rectangular and circular, can be purchased. Raising the beds to 60cm makes sowing seed, thinning or planting out seedling more convenient and general maintenance easier. As the soil level subsides, top up with a compost/manure mix.

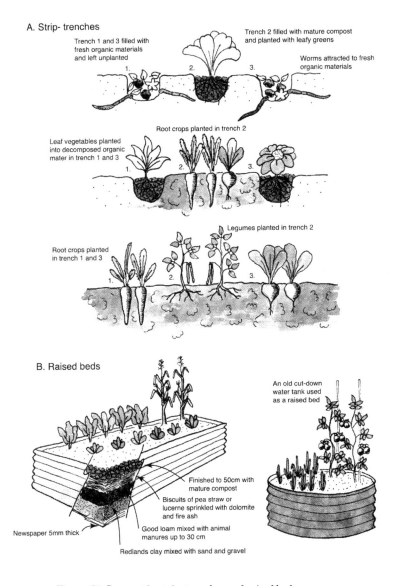

Figure 23. Compost in strip-trenches and raised beds

# How Do I Use Compost As Potting Mix?

Potting and seedling mix can be assembled using a fibrous compost with a high carbohydrate fraction to aid water retention. Fast-14 compost is ideal. Combine two parts of compost with one part of loam and one part of fine river sand. When sowing seed, fill seed punnets to 1cm from top, cover seed with finely sieved compost.

# Doesn't growing compost require a lot of space?

The answer is not necessarily! If there is a grass lawn, no matter how small, do you really need it? Is the maintenance of your lawn energy efficient? Could you cover the area with some other ground cover such as New Zealand spinach or pig face? Refer to Figure 24, opposite.

WEEDS are basically plants growing in the wrong place. Weeds with long tap roots 'mine' the sub-soil, concentrating mineral nutrients in their tissues as well as in the top-soil. At the same time, they aerate the soil and provide pathways for moisture. Provided a weed plant has not seeded, it can be thrown in with the compost. Marsh mallows are outstanding examples of a weed using the long tap roots (50 to 75cm long) for mining the soil. Dandelions also mine with their long tap roots, as well as being a compost activator. Added to these virtues, it is claimed that four fresh dandelion leaves every day will supply an adult with most of the essential vitamins and minerals. The ground, dried roots are used as a coffee substitute.

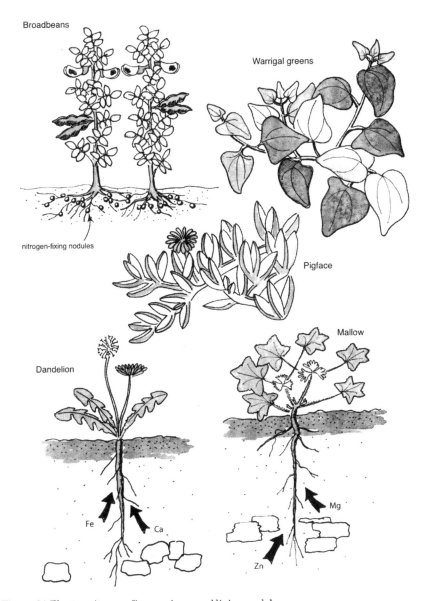

Broadbeans

nitrogen-fixing nodules

Warrigal greens

Pigface

Dandelion

Fe

Ca

Mallow

Mg

Zn

Figure 24. Plants - nitrogen fixers, miners and living mulchers

LEGUMES have nitrogen-accumulating bacteria in their root nodules, which enrich the soil as well as plant tissues. A patch of broad beans, soy beans or various peas will condition the soil, provide excellent compost as well as tasty spring vegetables. When removing plants, snip off at soil level, leaving roots with the nitrogenous nodules in the ground.

NEW ZEALAND SPINACH (*Tetragonia expansa*) grows along Southern Ocean shorelines. As its scientific name infers, it spreads, developing aerial roots, mulching as it stabilises sand dunes. Under it's synonym, Warragul Greens, it is listed as 'bush tucker'. It is an excellent spinach substitute when steamed. As it expands, it stifles weeds, builds up leaf litter and when too invasive can be thrown on the compost or fed to the chickens.

PIGFACE (*Carpobrotus spp.*) is a sprawling succulent, with mauve or yellow/orange flowers, has similar habitats and habits to New Zealand Spinach. Listed as 'bush tucker', the leaves can be cooked and the fruits eaten when soft, being sweet and juicy. Being a weed suppressive, salt and drought tolerant and a bush fire retardant, it is an excellent living mulch and ground cover. The grey kangaroos nibble at the edges of our pigface 'lawns; no doubt enjoying the salty taste.

HERBS—comfrey, borage, yarrow, tansy etc. as already stated have a role in the composting process as well as being of medicinal or culinary value.

## Any plant that grows in your garden is of nutritional value in your compost!

# THE A–Z OF
# COMPOST

# Accelerators and Activators

Compost accelerators speed up microbiological activity assisting decomposition processes such as fermentation (see Temperature). Fresh animal manures, grass clippings, liquid manure, seaweed extract, bran, molasses and yeast are all accelerators; so also are the herbs borage, comfrey, dandelion, stinging nettle and yarrow.

Commercial compost accelerators are available and considering their listed ingredients they are no doubt effective, but you can make up your own for a fraction of the cost.

### Here's one good recipe:

Make a hole in the compost heap and fill it with 5 parts grass clippings to 1 part fresh manure. Sprinkle with bran. Add 40 ml of seaweed extract and 250 ml of molasses to 10 litres of warm water. Mix well and pour mixture into the hole. Cover with more compost material.

It is cheapest to buy your bran and molasses from bulk health food stores and to take your own container for the molasses.

# Acidity/Alkalinity

See pH.

# Additives

Additives are minerals that supplement the nutrient content of the compost. They may be mineral chelates—as with the iron in stinging nettles and dandelion; the calcium, phosphate and potassium in comfrey leaves; or the array of nutrient minerals in seaweed and to a lesser extent molasses. The enzymes in these substances activate and accelerate the fermentation process whilst at the same time rapidly releasing the mineral supplements.

Additives may also be derived from wood ash, soot, bone meal and from rock flours and dusts. Rock supplements include calcium in limestone, calcium and magnesium in dolomite, phosphorus in phosphate rock and guano and potassium-rich granites and basalts. These rock substances tend to be 'slow release' additives, so add sparingly. Some of them are not easy to obtain but dolomite is available in small quantities from garden centres and in larger quantities from rural suppliers.

# Air

Air is essential to the composting process as it supplies oxygen for the aerobic (oxygen-absorbing) bacteria, which stimulate fermentation, glucose production and the fixing of nitrogen.

# Anaerobic Bacteria

Anaerobic Bacteria develop inside the heap, where there is no air. They heat the heap—an essential part of the decomposing process—and concentrate essential nutrients. Toss and turn the compost every third day, and the aerobic and anaerobic organisms will flourish alternately. Keep the heap moist. See also Temperature.

# Animal Manures

Animal Manures are very useful if not essential as compost. The best manures are produced by vegetarian animals. The grasses, grains and other vegetable matter are digested while the waste material is 'composted' within the animal in a perfect way. On excreting this waste, the aerobic (oxygen-absorbing) bacteria accelerate the composting process still further and the smell disappears.

Meat-eating animals produce very small amounts of manure compared to grazing animals. Excreta from dogs and cats may contain parasites and should not be added to composts.

Manures can be kept in either plastic bags or in a covered heap.

While fresh mature added to a compost heap will maximise its potency, only well-matured animal manures should be applied directly to soil. Manure is mature and ready for use when inhabited by earthworms. Their presence implies that the temperature is reasonable, aeration is good, moisture balanced and acidity/alkalinity neutral.

When applying manure to established trees, fork it around the drip line (where water drips from the outermost leaves).

Each type of manure has different qualities and contributes to particular functions within a plant. For more information see Chicken, Pigeon, Cow, Goat, Duck, Sheep, Pig and Horse Manure.

# Ants

Ants may invade dry heap, but will do no damage; in fact, they may help by aerating the heap. The ants will redistribute all the material, so the heap will not need to be tossed. The day before using ant-infested compost, water it well and the ants will leave.

# Application of Compost

When the temperature in your compost has dropped to the maximum daily air temperature, it is ready for use. If your compost has undergone sufficient heating, no seed will grow from it, but if you are sowing seed directly into it and you want to be absolutely sure, you can put it in the freezer for a couple of days. Compost covering sown seed should be sieved and well compacted.

When applying compost to flowerbeds, dig it in lightly with the existing soil. If the compost is mature, there should be no risk of it burning small plants, so don't worry if it touches the stalks.

Established shrubs and fruit trees will benefit from a ring of compost. Fork it in around the drip line, where water drips from the outermost leaves. Sprinkle this ring with dolomite and cover with a mulch of hay, straw or dried grass clippings. The fine roots will benefit from this as they grow outward and the ground will retain moisture in hot or windy weather. For direct planting into compost, see Strip trenching.

# Bacteria

Bacteria are by far the most abundant soil organism. They break down plant and animal residues in the compost, thereby releasing carbon dioxide, which plants absorb as gaseous vapours. Another vital role of bacteria is to convert organic nitrogen into ammonia and finally nitrates, which plants can then absorb through water. One group of bacteria fix nitrogen in the root nodules of legumes.

See also Anaerobic bacteria.

# Bananas

Banana skins, chopped, can be added to compost.

If you take over a garden that has a banana jungle in one corner, don't despair. You have a rich source of potassium, phosphorus and nitrogen. Once the plants are removed from the soil, split the stalks lengthwise with a spade or an axe. Cover the stalks up with some soil, carpet underfelt or plastic sheeting. They will take a few months to disintegrate. Add compost or animal manure and dolomite. This will provide you with a material to grow an abundance of cucubits—zucchini, squash and pumpkins.

# Bins and Boxes

The essential features of a compost bin or box are holes in the sides for air to enter and access for worms and other earth organisms at the base. Place boxes or bins on the soil. Very simple styles have advantages; a circle of wire mesh can be made in minutes and, when filled with compacted materials, lifted clear to start again. Cardboard cartons with a large hole in the base and holes cut in the sides provide a series of neat compost containers and they will eventually break down. Worms love cardboard.

More elaborate boxes can be made from bricks or timber. All compost containers should be covered on top.

Composting bins are available commercially and some municipal authorities are selling bins cheaply to encourage household composting.

# Biodynamic Method

A term coined by followers of Rudolf Steiner to suggest that the method harnesses biological energy to secure healthy soil.

# Blood and Bone

This is a commercial bi-product of slaughterhouses and butchers. Rich in phosphorus and nitrogen, bones have been a fertiliser source for centuries. During the nineteenth century Britain was accused of 'grave robbing' the battlefields of Europe in order to sustain her agriculture.

Today the bones are ground, dried blood is added and a bonemeal produced. Blood and bone can be extended by composting it with fibrous materials such as sawdust, lawn clippings or hay, or it can be applied directly onto soil, but be careful to sprinkle it away from young plants as it may 'burn' them. Many organic gardeners consider this to be an unhealthy product and avoid using it. It is possible that residues of chemical products and antibiotics remain in the blood and bone meal and are harmful to micro-organisms

# Borage

A herb closely related to comfrey, borage is also of great value to the compost as it develops massive succulent stalks, with many leaves and flowers. Chop with a spade and add to your heap.

# Boron (B)

Boron plays a vital role in flowering and fruiting. Seawater contains high levels of boron as it is concentrated in seaweed. Boron deficiency reduces the intake of other nutrient elements by the plants, which then become degenerate.

# Bran

Bran is the residue from refining or polishing wheat, rice or other grains. Bran contains a number of vitamins and enzymes and is a good source of NPK nutrients as well as iron.

It is an excellent compost accelerator but bees will swarm over bran if it is left uncovered. No doubt this is proof of its nutritional value. Bran is used as a poultry food and is available cheaply from health food stores.

# Calcium (Ca)

Calcium ensures plant maturity, high seed production and the intake of other essential elements. Although it occurs in relative abundance in the Earth's crust, calcium is in short supply or absent in soils derived purely from porous sandstone. Soils such as those of the Sydney region need a calcium supplement. Add ground limestone or preferably ground dolomite, which also helps adjust soil acidity by acting as a liming agent.

# Carbon and Carbon Dioxide (C and CO2)

Carbon atoms are the cornerstones of all molecules within plants. They form carbohydrates and the fibrous substance called cellulose. Carbon contributes to about 44% of dry plant material and is absorbed by plants in the gaseous form, carbon dioxide.

The decomposition of organic matter by the action of micro-organisms generates carbon dioxide. The carbon dioxide in turn fuels—or feeds—bacterial conversion of cellulose into glucose, which again produces carbon dioxide. This is an almost self-perpetuating system which is on-going in compost-making. As large amounts of carbon dioxide escape into the atmosphere, it is preferable to restrict air to the compost heap at times with a cover. When carbon dioxide is incorporated in water it forms a weak acid, carbonic acid. This acid dissolves soil-borne nutrients from humus, clay and mineral grains, making them ready for absorption by plants.

# Carbon-Nitrogen Balance

All organic matter contains both carbon and nitrogen in varying proportions. A vital function of composting is to convert carbon and nitrogen into plant food. The carbon content needs to be 25 times greater than the nitrogen content by weight, but should not be more than 30 times greater. This optimum ratio can be achieved by referring to The Carbon/Nitrogen Cone at the back of the book.

If there is too much carbon there will be a rapid production of methane, which will exhaust the carbohydrates before the nitrogen is converted biologically into ammonia. The resulting compost will be greatly reduced in volume, light in colour and nutrient deficient.

Too little carbon inhibits heating by microbial processes, thus slowing down decomposition. A dark, smelly mess results, due to an excess of ammonia. A varied diet is essential for your compost to become humus-rich, nitrogenous and friable. Refer also to Sulphur.

# Cardboard

Cardboard is a good mulching material but it needs a lot of dry material or compost on top to hold it in place until it is well soaked with water. It can also be composted, at the bottom of a heap or packed around the sides of a bin.

Worms love corrugated cardboard, so it must have good food value.

# Carpet Underfelt

Carpet layers will give you off-cuts of new underfelt and discarded old felt. Only those of natural fibre will decompose. Test the composition with a lighted match: if the threads melt then the felt is synthetic.

Underfelt can be used in various ways and when it finally breaks down it is a natural soil component. As a cover over a compost heap or box, it helps the heating and fermentation inside the heap, or use it to mulch around trees to keep weeds down and reduce evaporation.

A freshly composted garden bed can be covered with underfelt. To plant out seedlings cut holes in the felt and plant directly into the compost beneath.

To sow seed, cut slits in cardboard and lay a fine layer of compost in the slits. This is a water- and nutrient-retaining system, particularly good in sandy, coastal or arid inland soils.

# Cartons

Cartons are also good for seed planting. When the seedlings are ready to plant out, cut the bottom of the carton away and put the rest in the soil or under mulch. In this way the seedling is not disturbed and the carton will weather away.

Milk and other drink cartons can be composted but they take a long time—many months. Their only residue is a fine film of plastic from the outside. But they are a nuisance in a compost heap, so give them a small corner of their own with some leaves or grass

# Chamomile

Rich in calcium, chamomile is a good additive to compost and it subdues smells, keeping the compost sweet. The herb is worth growing as it is known as the plant doctor, helping many plants and the soil to keep healthy.

# Charcoal

Charcoal is a residue from wood fires. It is mineral rich and so of value in compost. It can be separated from wood ash in water, since charcoal floats. It is a very porous material and acts like a sponge for nutrients dissolved in water. If you leave charcoal in a liquid manure or tea, for example, it will act as a slow-release plant food when incorporated in garden beds.

Charcoal is also a valuable addition to potting mix, improving drainage and aeration, as well as being a nutrient source. Plant roots seek out this enrichment and can be seen growing into the charcoal.

# Chelates (pronounced Kee-lates)

Chelates are organic compounds that have attracted inorganic metals into their structures. Chelate means claw-like and this gives a picture of the process. In bonding with stable organic substances, the metallic element becomes available in the soil for plant absorption.

Our own health also requires chelated elements. We cannot cure anaemia by swallowing iron filings. Even our absorption of iron from various inorganic salts is pitifully slow, but when iron is bonded into organic amino acid compounds, rapid absorption takes place.

Mineral elements in the soil are congregated by chelation with organic compounds. This applies particularly to the trace elements iron, copper, boron and manganese. Chelates are water soluble and stable and so are readily converted into plant tissue.

Composting produces chelates. Earthworms and all organic material added to the soil have chelating properties. Mosses and lichens attached to apparently barren rocks will survive by producing chelating substances, which dissolve rocks to release micronutrients. This chelating mechanism permits lichen to grow in such hostile environments as ice-free rock surfaces in the Antarctic.

Foods such as molasses, yeast, yoghurt and buttermilk are rich in a wide range of chelated mineral nutrients and are thus excellent compost additives and accelerators.

To see how iron may be chelated from the soil by compost or mulch, see Iron.

# Chicken Manure

Chicken manure contains a good balance of NPK nutrients. All bird excreta is highly concentrated as the nitrogen-rich urea is combined with the solids and not voided as a liquid.

The high phosphate content is excellent for fruiting vegetables, such as tomatoes, but the manure must not be applied fresh, as ammonia is given off and will harm plants.

Mature fresh chicken manure in a heap can be covered with soil or vegetable matter to conserve valuable nitrates. When worms invade the heap the manure is mature. This should take less than a month. Bird droppings lack roughage, so to retain moisture mix with hay, sawdust or shredded paper.

The domestic hen is an efficient producer of compost when housed on deep litter and fed on vegetable scraps and grain. This litter of hay or straw is turned constantly by the bird, which each year gives 10 kg of manure and, of course, eggs. For suburban gardens, bustling little bantams are ideal and make very charming pets. Kept on deep litter, there are almost no smells or flies.

Pelletised poultry manure is commercially available. Another poultry manure, Dynamic Lifter, has an excellent reputation. It is a concentrated organic fertiliser, produced by a composting method. It is processed under chemically controlled conditions so that the ammonia compounds are converted into benign nitrates with concentrations of other nutrients and trace elements.

# Chlorine (Cl)

Although it is an essential trace element, chlorine is seldom lacking in soil as vegetation and rainfall supply sufficient amounts.

# Clover

Clover is a spreading legume that fixes nitrogen and acts as a living mulch, retaining moisture in the soil and inhibiting weed growth. The growing clover mat also increases the earthworm population by providing cover and nutrient. At the same time the worms aerate the soil, enhancing the clover's soil-enriching functions. Red and white clovers can be sown from seed and are available from health food stores. When grown, the clover can be cut and added to the compost, either as green manure, or dried as a hay. The roots, left in position, enrich the soil with nitrogen.

In Australia, the CSIRO has refined this natural process by developing 'Clever Clover'. The clover dies down in spring but self-seeds with regrowth in autumn. This system is sustainable horticulture at its best. It is also a great example of 'no dig' gardening, as crop seedlings are planted into the mat of spent clover in late spring.

# Coffee Grounds

Coffee grounds are high in proteins and oils, which makes them good micro-organism food—perfect for the compost.

Don't apply them directly to growing plants as they will wilt with the rancid aroma.

In the industrial process, after the essentials are extracted from coffee beans to produce instant coffee, the residues become waste. If you can, get a quantity of this waste from a factory.

# Comfrey

The succulent leaves of this herb are rich in calcium, phosphorus, potassium and vitamins A, C and B12. Chop the leaves with a spade and add them to the heap. Alternatively, make a liquid tea with them and apply it directly to your soil, diluted with 5 parts water.

See also Liquid manures and teas.

# Compost Water

Compost water is a revitalising fertiliser for house plants and window and balcony boxes. Soak well matured compost in water for several hours. When water is coloured, decant liquid and apply directly to roots. Compost water can be run off from modern compost bins, such as AEROBIN. The biocycle system automatically distributes waste water (refer to figure 20).

# Contaminants and pollutants

If the sources of composting materials are unknown they may contain contaminants. These may inhibit the biological activity, that is so essential to the satisfactory maturation of the compost, and may affect the vegies to be grown in it.

Contaminants and pollutants can be inorganic substances, such as sulphur, lead or cadmium. See Paper, Sulphur, and Trace elements.

The major concern, however, is with toxic organics: insecticides, herbicides and fungicides. These may be present as residues in a range of plant wastes, sawdust, hay and straw. Animal manures from factory farming may contain such residues and, in addition, the effects from hormone and antibiotic treatments may upset microbial action in compost.

On the positive side of all this is the fact that composting will break down many of these substances. If the earthworms keep away from a mature compost, then there is a problem.

You don't always know what you are bringing into your garden. In our community garden hundreds of bags of grass clippings were received each year from a mowing contractor. These were emptied into a heap on their own and many bags had a strong chemical smell. The heap was tossed every two or three days and the chemical smell quickly diminished. After only eight to ten days the resulting dark, friable material was used as a mulch without any ill effects on the plants.

# Composting Worms

A species of earthworm, composting ideal for humus production; sometimes called vermicomposting.

# Cooking Oil and Fats

Since these are organic, they will compost. It is best to pour them into a hole in your compost and cover to avoid flies, etc.

# Copper (Cu)

Copper is present in a number of enzymes and probably plays a catalytic role in plant respiration and utilisation of iron. It can be maintained at the desired level by applications of grass clippings, sawdust or seaweed to the compost.

# Cow Manure

Cattle are very efficient digesters of vegetation, especially fibrous grasses and hay. Their composting vessel is known as a rumen.

Here food is worked over by myriad bacteria and other micro-organisms.

Cellulose is reduced by enzymal action to a pulp and regurgitated for a further chewing. It then passes through the true stomach for final digestion. This is a highly adapted and efficient cellulose-splitting system and takes eighteen days to complete.

The fresh manure contains nutrients and an array of micro-organisms. Their function changes when the anaerobic environment within the animal is exchanged for the aerobic state of the paddock.

The whole digestive and elimination process is so efficient that little of the food taken in by the beast is passed out as manure but being rich in both micro¬organisms and enzymes, cow manure is very beneficial in compost and is an excellent worm food. It also makes a valuable liquid manure.

Pelletised cow manure is available commercially. The product has been kiln dried and it is not clear whether the enzymes and bacteria can be revitalised when water is added to reconstitute the manure.

# Dandelion

In their growing process, dandelions absorb two to three times more iron than any other plant. Iron is a trace element and also an activator. Dandelions can be added as whole plants or as a liquid tea.

# Dolomite

Dolomite aids biochemical processes in plant growth. It is a rock that has usually been formed in shallow seas or estuaries. It is not only a liming material and a soil conditioner, but it is a contributor of calcium and magnesium to the soil.

Being formed in seawater it also contains other vital concentrated trace elements, such as manganese, boron and iron. As many Australian soil types are deficient in these nutrients, dolomite provides an excellent supplement to the soil or to a mature compost.

Application of dolomite is essential for growing fruit and vegetables on porous sandstone soils, such as those of the Sydney region. Citrus trees benefit if dolomite is added to compost, mulch or manure being spread around them.

# Duck Manure

This manure is rich in nitrogen and phosphorus, so it is a very valuable product. The sloppy nature of the manure and the tendency of the birds to 'duck under' fences and gates and go travelling makes duck-keeping a difficult proposition in suburban gardens.

# Dynamic Lifter

See Chicken manure.

# Earthworms

There are a number of native Australian earthworms, including the spectacular Giant Gippsland Earthworm, but most garden worms have emigrated to Australia in pot plants The earthworms in your compost feed on vegetable and animal refuse and expel casts. These casts are a valuable manure on their own. They contain micro-organisms, rich in NPK and other nutrients and are bound together by biochemically complex mucus. Remarkably, trace elements not discernible in your soil, may be present in worm castsin that soil. Worm casts are even marketed as a liquidmanure (see Liquid Manures and Teas).

Earthworms are reliable indicators of pollution. If earthworms keep away from compost materials which have been kept moist and covered for some weeks, the heap contains something toxic.

If your garden is totally lacking in earthworms, they can be ordered by mail from worm farms.

Famed for his controversial work *On the Origin of Species*, Charles Darwin did valuable fieldwork on earthworms, over a period of many years. He wrote, 'it may be doubted whether there are any other animals which have played so important a part in the history of the world...'. He described them as 'Nature's ploughshare' and concluded that all the vegetable mould in England has passed and will pass, time and time again, through the intestinal tract of earthworms.

# Eggshells

Eggshells break down quickly and provide lime to a compost. Also the membrane inside the shell contains a complexity of organic molecules on which bacteria multiply once the shell is broken. Organic acids from nitrogenous material dissolve the alkaline eggshells, which in turn neutralise the acids.

# Elements

Sixteen elements are present within all vegetable matter and are placed below in one of three groups. From these figures it is apparent that essential elements are more abundant than major elements, which in turn are present in much higher concentrations than trace elements.

Approximate percentage of each element is by weight in dry plant matter.

ESSENTIAL ELEMENTS

Carbon (C) 44% Oxygen (0) 44% Hydrogen (H) 6 %

MAJOR ELEMENTS

Nitrogen (N) 1.5% Potassium (K) 1.5% Phosphorus (P) 0.2%

Calcium (Ca) 0.2% Magnesium (Mg) 0.2% Sulphur (S) 0.2%

TRACE ELEMENTS

Chlorine (Cl) 0.1% Iron (Fe) 0.01% Manganese (Mn) 0.01% Zinc (Zn) 0.004% Copper (Cu) 0.0003% Boron (B) 0.0003% Molybdenum (Mo) 0.00015%

Deficiencies in any of these elements show up in the developing plant. The function of each of these elements is dealt with separately and further information can be found under Nutrients, Trace elements and NPK.

# Elephant Manure

There is an urban myth about the vitality transmitted to plants by elephant manure. The circus is eagerly awaited—to collect the elephant droppings. In nutrient and vitamin content this manure is no more valuable than horse manure, but it has one advantage: the size and cohesion of the pats make them easier to collect

# Enzymes

These are complex biochemical molecules that stimulate specific organic functions. Without enzymes plants could not grow, seed or reproduce; vegetable matter could not decompose, microbiological cycles would not operate and earthworms could not collect and concentrate nutrients, particularly nitrogen, phosphorus and potassium, in their casts.

Enzymes help activate photosynthesis and oxygen transfer within the plant. They speed up the fixation of nitrogen from the atmosphere but they are not part of the micro-organisms doing this work, nor are they contained in the molecular structure which uses the nitrogen. So the role of the enzyme seems elusive but it is a vital character in the plant life scenario.

# Fish

The value of fish in the soil was understood long ago, when South American Incas planted their corn seed directly into a hole on top of a sardine head. Fish bones and dried fish meal have a high nutrient content, especially of phosphate. All fish material should be buried deep in the compost and covered. with soil, sawdust, grass clippings or plastic

See also Shellfish, Sea water and Seaweed.

# Fruit

Residues from juicing fruit are valuable in compost (see Uses and Values Table at the back of the book). Many people think that citrus fruits are too acid and keep them out of the compost heap.

# Fruit Fly

Fruit flies are the spoilers of summer fruits in many parts of Australia, particularly along the east coast.

The wasp-like fly lays eggs in the unripe fruit. Larvae develop as whitish maggots and burrow throughout the fruit.

Do not add infested fruit to your compost. To rid the fruit of flies, either boil fruit or collect it in a plastic bag, seal and place in the sun. Only when the maggots and flies are dead is it safe to add to the compost. Fruit fly infestation is a serious problem and we should all work towards its eradication.

# Fungi

Fungi are just one component in the great assembly of soil micro-organisms. They are constantly at work in the compost heap, producing nutritious humus from plant residues. Fungi form networks of white threads in your compost heap and occasionally toadstools and mushrooms.

# GAIA Theory

Developed by James Lovelock (refer Lovelock 2009 & refs therein). The theory considers the earth as a self regulating system, integrating living organisms, with the surface crust, oceans and the atmosphere. This theory falls within the scientific field of biogeochemistry. Composting, whether natural or contrived, adheres to this theory.

# Garden Waste

Any plant refuse from the garden can be composted. The rapidity of decomposition is greatly increased by chopping with a spade or by putting the waste through a muncher or shredder. See Shredder and munchers, Grass clippings, Leaves and Weeds.

# Goat Manure

Goat manure is very similar to sheep manure in form, composition and use as a fertiliser. I have not used goat manure mysekf. It may have special attributes in addition to those of sheep manure.

We do know that goat manure stimulates oil production in fruits and herbs. Visualise the goats grazing on rosemary and oregano amongst the olive groves on some steep Mediterranean shore.

# Grass Clippings

A massive volume of grass is mown each week from Australian lawns. Grass clippings are a fantastic fuel in which to digest other plant wastes. In a pile they heat up rapidly, producing carbon dioxide, which in turn activates the process of nitrogen fixation by bacteria.

If a compost collection is developing slowly, accelerate it by adding the same volume of fresh grass clippings and covering the heap for a week or so. If you have no grass to mow for clippings, your neighbours or a mowing contractor will probably be glad to supply them.

# Green Manures

Green manures do not just rest the soil, they revitalise it, particularly over winter. The most important function of a green manure is below the soil surface. The mass of roots stabilises against soil erosion, aerates the soil, brings up nutrients from deep down and finally provides organic material when cut and added to the compost.

Legumes make particularly good green manures as their root nodules fix atmospheric nitrogen. They are pod bearers and include the whole range of beans, peas, clovers, lucernes, alfalfa, lupins and fenugreek. In addition to their function as green manures, most of these plants will give you a crop to enjoy.

Non-leguminous green manures include barley, rye grass, oats, millet, wheat, buckwheat, comfrey and borage. Bird seed, available from supermarkets, is also a good source of green manure. Try the one labelled Wild Bird Seed: it produces an interesting range of grains.

Harvest green manures before the plants die, leaving the roots in the ground and delivering the rest to your compost.

A range of good green manures grow from seed, available from New Gippsland Seed Farm, P.O. Box 1, Silvan 3795, and some sprouters, such as alfalfa, can be bought from health food shops.

# Guano

The dried excreta of birds and bats forms guano-phosphate-rich accumulations, built up over a long period. Probably the best guano is that from seabirds as it contains a range of trace elements present in seawater. Once deposited on limestone rocks, a mineralisation process takes place. This hardens and becomes phosphate rock

Most Australian soils are lacking in phosphorus and for many years guano was the only source of enrichment available. The industry was very destructive in its exploitation of this phosphate rock on several groups of islands, such as the Abrolhos and Recherche Islands and those in the Bass Strait; also cave deposits on the mainland were mined, destroying bat roosts.

# Hair, Wool and Feathers

Human hair from the hairdresser's floor is a high nitrogen source as it contains one sixth of its weight in nitrogen. The same is true for animal hair, wool and bird feathers.

# Hay

Hay is a compost extender and a material for mulch. The nutrient quality of the hay varies considerably. Lucerne, alfalfa and clover hays, being legumes, have a higher nitrogen content than wheaten or oaten hays.

See Legumes and Nitrogen.

# Horse Manure

Horses are not ruminants like cows and sheep. Feed passes through them fairly rapidly and the fresh dung is moist, not dehydrated like sheep droppings. A countryman who had a low opinion of horse manure once described it as 'all piss and straw' and indeed it is the least nutritious of the animal manures.

In spite of this, horse manure is a useful composting material, makes an excellent mulch and acts as a binder in very sandy soil. The binding property is illustrated by the fact that horse manure added to clay makes good mud bricks.

As stabled racehorses are given high protein feed some people consider this dung to be the best source of horse manure, but it may contain substances toxic to soil biology (see Contaminants and pollutants).

# Human Wastes

In Australia a great amount of precious, fresh water is used to sweep human wastes through sewage systems and out to sea. Alternative household methods of disposal are becoming recognised by health authorities.

The Rota-Loo composts human wastes without using water. A small heater in the system evaporates fluids and a fan draws the vapour, through a vent pipe, into the atmosphere. The collecting tank below the toilet floor has four chambers which are rotated as each fills. The solid waste in the chambers slowly converts to an odourless humus, low in nitrogen and free of toxins. By the time the fourth chamber is in use, the first is thoroughly composted and may be removed and its contents buried in the earth.

The Biolet works on the same principle and requires little installation, only a vent pipe and a small fan heater.

Properties which process sewage and household waste water through a septic system can now discharge the fluids onto the land, as shown in the diagram. We are nourishing a young orchard in this way. All these systems, of course, require council approval.

# Humic Acid

The generic term for a complexity of organic acids, including amino-acids, released during the humification process. These acids redistribute nitrogen compounds into the soil.

# Humus

Humus is a lightweight, loose, dark-coloured material that acts as a sponge to retain water and nutrients. It is the ideal end-product of composting. It will prevent soil from compacting, maintain a pH balance and support soil organisms, including earthworms.

A slow compost, taking a few months to mature, should contain humus. The rapid composts made in tumblers or by the Fast Fourteen recipe will not achieve the final humic stage but they will contain the elements necessary to nourish the soil and in time will form humus in the soil.

# Hydrogen (H)

Hydrogen is one of the three essential elements for plant food, with oxygen and carbon. Plants extract hydrogen from water.

# Indore Method

This method of composting was developed in India by Sir Alfred Howard (1947). It consists of systematic layering of highly nitrogenous material sandwiched between fibrous carbon rich plant debris.

# Insects

Any infestation of insects in your compost heap or bin is an indication of imbalance. The presence of ants or caterpillars means the compost is too dry. Cockroaches and maggots know that their food is available and the temperature low enough for them to flourish. Heat the heap rapidly by adding grass clippings or hay.

Flies are attracted by emissions of gases, so cover compost with soil, carpet underfelt or plastic sheeting. See also Ants, Mice, Slaters, slugs and snails.

# Iron (Fe)

Iron gives leaves and grasses their depth of colour. Lacking iron they tend to be yellow—anaemic, as we become when we need iron. In fact the function of iron in oxygen transfer in plants can be compared to the association of iron with haemoglobin in our bloodstream. Iron is the catalyst to carry oxygen to the leaves of plants for the synthesis of chlorophyll, the substance that gives plants their green colour.

Due to a succession of arid periods in Australia's geological history, iron is present in most soils. Various iron ochres colour the soils in hues of red, brown, orange or yellow. From these iron oxides the iron is not in a form available to plants, but iron molecules from the soil can be attracted into organic compounds by the process of chelation. This process regulates iron intake and will occur naturally when there is an abundance of humus.

The chelation process can be observed where a thick mat of mulch or compost covers a red or orange clay soil but is not dug in. At first there will be a sharp line between the soil and the cover. Gradually the soil colour will lose its intensity. It will be more brown, then grey brown at the surface layer. In this way trace amounts of iron are made available for plant intake.

See Elements and Chelates.

# Kitchen Wastes

Kitchen wastes are often highly nitrogenous but used alone they have insufficient carbon to fuel the composting process. If the decomposition of kitchen waste is not rapid, this protein-rich material will smell bad. It will become food for pests rather than for micro-organisms that create compost. So it is essential to mix it with carbonaceous materials, such as hay, grass clippings, shredded paper and sawdust.

See also Cooking oils and fats, Meat scraps, Fish and Shellfish

# Leaves

Leaves of many plants and trees, especially the Australian eucalypts, decompose very slowly and they are deficient in nitrogen. So a leaf mulch used around trees and shrubs will keep weeds and grass down. It looks good but needs building up from time to time.

Leaves to be composted should be mixed with other wastes. A suitable mixture is two parts (by weight) grass clippings, three parts weeds and one part leaves. Shredding speeds up the rotting process.

# Legumes

Legumes are pod-bearers. They are also nitrogen-fixing factories, gathering nitrogen by means of bacteria in root nodules. In addition, the deep roots of legumes bring up nutrients, including trace elements, from the sub-soil.

They provide us with bean and pea seeds to eat; flowers for the house, such as lupins and sweet peas; and fodder for stock, including clover, alfalfa and lucerne hay. All these plants are valuable in compost.

See also Clover, Green manure, Hay, Living mulch and Nitrogen.

# Liming

Lime is applied to reduce soil acidity. It sweetens the soil, introduces valuable nutrients and conditions the soil for proper water percolation.

One form of lime is ground limestone (calcium carbonate) but the best is ground dolomite (magnesium calcium carbonate). Following dolomite application, weak acids in the soil release carbon dioxide from the rock flour, leaving behind the alkaline hydroxides of calcium and magnesium. This natural chemical reaction works on a large scale over a long-time span to form caves in limestone country.

Limestone or dolomite can be applied directly to soil at the time of planting seedlings or sowing seed. It is best to add them to compost at the end of the composting process as they may otherwise adversely affect the bacterial cycles.

Another form, slaked lime (hydrate of calcium) must be applied two weeks before planting seedlings or sowing seed and should not be added to compost while it is working. It is not a natural product and can damage the roots of plants.

Wood ash also acts as a liming substance.

Liming is hardly necessary in limestone areas along the southern coast of Australia but it is essential for the sandstone soils of the Sydney area, which are very acid and lacking in calcium and magnesium.

The beneficial nutrients from liming are discussed under Dolomite and Wood ash.

# Liquid Manures and Teas

In small gardens where it may be impractical to make compost, liquid manures and teas are invaluable. Comfrey alone contains so many nutrients that, as a tea, it may keep a garden in good health without any animal manure at all.

Animal manures, seaweed, comfrey leaves, dandelions, stinging nettles, yarrow and molasses are all very beneficial. To make a tea, lay the substance in a closed container and cover with plenty of rainwater. Stir every day or so. After three weeks it should be ready to use. Concentrated worm-cast liquid manure is available commercially, under names such as 'Worm Drops'.

Liquid manures and teas may be applied, diluted, directly to plants or added to the compost as Accelerators.

# Living Mulch

Living mulches are plants that feed us and the soil. Sweet potato vines mulch the ground while their roots swell to form edible tubers. Creeping legume vines, like lab lab beans (*Dolithos lablab*) and rice beans (*Vigna umbeliata*), provide mulch and edible pods and their root nodules fix nitrogen. These vines spread rapidly and so they are only useful where a large area of ground is available.

New Zealand spinach (*Tetragonia expansa*) is more controllable. It is a natural seashore stabiliser with succulent leaves which mulches readily and makes an excellent hot-weather substitute for spinach. These seeds are available from Eden Seeds, MS 905, Beechmont Qld 4211.

CSIRO in Australia has developed the ultimate in living mulch. It is an inedible mulch called 'Clever Clover' (see Clover).

# Magnesium (Mg)

Magnesium is critical for plant development. Without it there would be no green plants. Magnesium is one of the catalysts in the production of chlorophyll, the substance that greens leaves. It also assists in water regulation, absorption of nitrogen, phosphorus and sulphur, and helps in the formation of proteins and other biochemical complexes.

Ground dolomite rock rectifies a magnesium deficiency. It also provides supplementary calcium and is a liming substance, adjusting acidity in the soil. The sandstone soils of Sydney and its surrounds are deficient in magnesium, so dolomite is an essential ingredient added to soil or to compost.

# Manganese (Mn)

This element is involved in the photosynthetic process. Though present in most soils, it has to be converted into soluble chelate salts so that it is available to plants. This is achieved by microbiological activity. Seaweed, lucerne or other legume hays will contribute ample manganese to a diverse compost mixture.

# Manures

See Animal manures.

# Meat Scraps

Provided your compost is working and the temperature in the centre is high, you can add meat scraps to it. Make a hole in the centre and put the scraps in, then cover with a handful of sawdust or grass clippings. The heat should 'cook' any maggots and the cover will protect the compost from flies, etc.

# Mice

If mice burrow or make nests in your compost, it shows that protein foods are not being broken down. The heap needs to be revitalised with the addition of heat-producing materials, such as grass clippings. A dramatic increase in temperature will persuade the mice to move. A cat would remove the mice but it can't assist in maturing the compost. Pests are an indicator that all is not well with the digesting process in the heap.

# Micro-organisms

These include algae, bacteria, fungi, protozoa and yeasts. Simplistic in form yet complex in their biochemical interactions, they form a microcosm within the soil. Their life and work creates and maintains soil in a way that sustains plants.

Micro-organisms assist in making elements acceptable for plant intake. They concentrate minerals and link them with organic compounds to form chelates. The chelating process is so powerful that it can corrode rock into soil.

Temperature, moisture, aeration, and pH dictate micro-biological activity in the soil. When conditions are just right for a particular group of organisms, its population will develop explosively. For example, when compost is tossed and aired the anaerobic bacteria that flourish in a closed heap will be almost instantaneously replaced by an aerobic population.

Approximate quantity of micro-organisms to each gram of soil:

| | |
|---|---|
| algae | 100 000 |
| bacteria | 1 000 000 000 |
| fungi | 1 000 000 |
| protozoa | 1 000 000 |
| yeasts | 1 000 |

# Molasses

A residue from the process of refining cane sugar, molasses is a wonderful chelator.

Mix one cup of molasses in 10 litres of warm rainwater and sprinkle onto the accumulated compost. Cover it up or your heap may be visited by a swarm of bees. The resulting acceleration of the fermentation process is exciting—measure it daily with a thermometer.

Molasses can be obtained cheaply from bulk health food stores; take your own container.

# Molybdenum (Mo)

Of all the trace elements molybdenum is absorbed by plants in the most minute amounts, yet it is a vital element, a catalyst in the bacterial activity of fixing atmospheric nitrogen.

The leguminous hays, alfalfa, clover and lucerne contain enriched concentrations of moly. Seaweeds also have significant quantities.

The minute dose of moly required by plants can be satisfied by a balanced compost, both in terms of constituents and the acidity-alkalinity scale (see pH). A deficiency of this element is probably due to an acid soil and can be rectified by liming.

# Mulch

Grass clippings, hay or straw can be used, also newspaper and cardboard, pinned down by weights. These materials will eventually join the soil but as mulches they are nutrient deficient. As they are totally aerated, developing gases escape and there is no anaerobic phase to concentrate nutrients.

You can spread mulch around young plants that are developing well and some seedlings can be planted directly into mulch, provided they have enough soil surrounding their roots. Potatoes thrive in deep mulch. As their roots grow sideways rather than downwards, mulch can be added as the plant grows. In this way the greening of potatoes is prevented. Potatoes exposed to the sun develop the greening substance, solanine, to which many people are allergic.

Carpet underfelt can be used as a water- and nutrient-retaining mulch for vegetable growing in arid sandy soils, such as coastal sand dunes.

For more on mulches, see Living mulch and Clover.

# Newsprint Ink

Newsprint ink is now totally synthetic, containing no mineral or other toxic components. Therefore newspapers can be added freely to compost. The coated coloured paper from glossy magazines also contain no toxic ink but take longer to decompose than newspaper.

# Nitrogen (N)

Nitrogen stimulates leaf growth as well as helping to feed the plant. It ensures seed fertility and reproductive fidelity through genetic imprinting.

Nitrogen is a vital plant nutrient. It is the linchpin in many biochemical molecules, including all proteins, amino acids, chlorophyll and the DNA molecules.

Gaseous nitrogen occupies four-fifths of Earth's atmosphere, yet it cannot be absorbed directly into cells or tissue. It can only be absorbed when 'fixed' in combination with other elements. Some of this fixation occurs due to electrical storms, but mostly it is through microbiological activity in the decomposition of natural materials.

Nitrogen can combine with hydrogen to form gaseous ammonia and in the composting process this gas should be confined to the inside of the heap. If you get the smells associated with fresh manures, cover the heap with more material or soil—you are wasting a product that will later become a valuable nitrate.

Nitrogen can combine with other nutrients, say potassium and oxygen, to form potassium nitrate. Such nitrates are readily soluble and can be absorbed by plants.

Legumes fix large amounts of nitrogen from the atmosphere by root bacteria contained in root nodules, often visible to the naked eye (see Legumes, also Green manures and Clover). Experiments on this phenomena in the USA found that over a ten-year period nitrogen fixed by alfalfa = 281 kg per hectare, red clover = 188 kg per hectare, soya beans = 118 kg per hectare and field peas 54 kg per hectare.

# NPK

This refers to the chemical abbreviations for Nitrogen—N, Phosphorus—P and Potassium—K, which are the major plant nutrients. Nitrogen stimulates leaf growth. Phosphorus enhances seed and fruit formation. Potassium strengthens stems, increases root growth and helps in the setting of fruit.

The proportions of NPK in artificial fertilisers vary according to the application. For example, a rose fertiliser has an NPK balance differing from a citrus or lawn food. Such precision cannot be achieved with organic fertilisers. A properly developed compost, however, is a complete plant food. If such composts are applied to a garden regularly, plant problems of all kinds should diminish.

# Nutrients

Plants absorb nutrients from the air and from the soil. With these nutrients they make a complexity of organic molecules, which, in specific combinations enable plants to flourish. These include glucose, cellulose, proteins, essential oils, amino acids, vitamins and chlorophyll—all substances vital for plant growth and reproduction.

The essential elements carbon, oxygen and hydrogen—are absorbed by plants as gaseous vapours. The other thirteen elements are transmitted to the plant from the soil, compost, mulch or manure. While mulches are usually nutrient deficient, they do hold moisture which is essential to the process of nutrient intake by plants.

Any soil, however nutrient rich it may be, needs to be revitalised as plants constantly draw nutrients from it. Composts and manures bear the raw materials from which nutrients are derived, so apply them regularly and you will get striking results from your garden.

# Oxygen (O)

One of the three essential elements present in all vegetable matter is oxygen. Plants absorb oxygen both directly from the atmosphere and through chemical reactions involving water or water vapour. See also Elements.

# Paper

This is an excellent compost extender; it works best if applied torn up. Wetted paper also makes a good mulch if weighted down. Paper mulching retains moisture and multiplies earthworm activity around trees. (See Newsprint ink)

# pH

Traditionally, soil that tasted sour or bitter was regarded as unsuitable for growing crops. Sour soils were too acid and bitter soils too alkaline. A sweet- tasting soil was known to be fertile.

Today we measure soil acidity and alkalinity in terms of pH units; pH stands for the power of hydrogen and is the relationship between hydrogen ions (H+) and hydroxyl ions (OH–). The more hydrogen ions the greater the acidity, whilst hydroxyl ions dominate in alkaline environments.

The pH scale is from 1 (extremely acid) to 14 (extremely alkaline). A balance is achieved at 7, which is termed neutral. The optimum pH for the majority of common plants is between 6.5 and 7. At this level soils will support the full range of microbiological activity favourable for healthy plant growth.

Note that the pH range for the ornamental shrubs is not compatible with that for the more common vegetables.

pH testers are commercially available and you may find them advertised in garden magazines or at your local garden centre.

# Phosphate Rock

Most phosphate rock imported into Australia comes from tropical islands. Over many centuries seabirds have deposited their excreta, their bones and their feathers, to react with coral limestone. The result is a phosphate rock with varying degrees of hardness (see Guano).

Phosphate rock is barely soluble in water, but if the rock is ground to a powder, organic humic acids in the soil will release phosphorus. This powdered phosphate rock contains a range of trace elements from the diet of the seabirds. It is a terrific compost supplement, especially as RPR (reactive phosphate rock), which has been heat treated to increase solubility, is so absorbable by plants. Available on order from garden and rural suppliers.

# Phosphorus (P)

Phosphorus is a vital element in all biological energy transfer systems, such as the conversion of solar energy into chemical energy with the formation of chlorophyll and glucose. It encourages fruit development and fertility of the resultant seed. Bones and other skeletal material, such as prawn shells, are rich in phosphorus. Other phosphorus sources are from accumulations of animal manure; seabirds in particular but also bats. Earthworm casts are also rich in phosphorus.

See Blood and bone, Shellfish, Phosphate rock and Guano

# Photosynthesis

Plants, algae and certain bacteria are distinguished from all other organisms by the biochemical process called photosynthesis. It is a complexity of reactions which convert solar energy into chemical energy in the presence of carbon dioxide and water for the manufacture of cell materials. The carbon dioxide is generated by the decaying of vegetation in the composting process.

# Pig Manure

Pig manure is reputed to strengthen root development and is particularly good for potatoes, sweet potatoes and other tuber crops. It must be well composted.

# Pigeon Manure

This is the richest form of manure produced by domestic animals. Use as for chicken manure. If you can only collect a small amount, put it in a container with rain-water, cover and leave for three weeks. Dilute the mixture and use as a liquid manure.

# Plastics

Few plastics are biodegradable but thick plastic sheeting is excellent for covering the compost heap. It keeps the flies out, holds moisture and odours in, and prevents nutrients escaping in the form of gases. In heavy rain an uncovered heap becomes soggy and bacterial action is set back.

Plastic bags make good containers in which to render weeds and even fruit flies harmless. Seal tightly and leave in the sun until contents have decomposed.

# Potassium (K)

Potassium is a major plant nutrient in the form of potash (K20). Although it does not occur within plant-forming molecules, it is involved in complex biochemical interactions, such as starch, sugar and protein formation, and in photosynthesis. It increases root growth, strengthens stems and assists in setting fruit and brilliance of flower colour.

Potassium is contained in most organic materials, although some, such as wood ash, soot and seaweed, are richer than others. Other potassium-rich minerals are granite and basalt rock flours, so if your soil is of granite or basalt origin, you will not have a potash deficiency.

Commercial fertilisers usually contain potassium chloride. Such potash salts are so readily soluble that they may cause the plant to absorb excess potash, which can inhibit assimilation of other nutrients, such as phosphorus. This problem does not occur in organic sources as the intake of nutrients by the plant is both slower and more balanced.

# Potting and Seedling mix

Mix three parts well-matured compost with one part fine, washed sand. Cover seeds with sieved compost, not sand. Charcoal can be used for drainage; it also absorbs nutrients that are released again through watering. If you are concerned about harmful organisms in your mixture, put it in the deep freeze for a few days.

# Rockflours and Dust

Granite and basalt rocks have a high potassium content and may contain significant traces of calcium, magnesium and phosphorus, depending on their origin. They are an excellent compost supplement if applied in a powdered form. A monumental mason might be prepared to supply you, or you can order through garden suppliers.

For comments on rock nutrients see Potassium, Phosphate rock and Dolomite.

# Rocking Horse Manure

See URINE.

# Sawdust

Saw-mills and joineries produce a lot of sawdust. It is mainly composed of cellulose and has a high carbon/low nitrogen content (see The Carbon/Nitrogen Cone, figure 8). To compensate, compost sawdust with highly nitrogenous materials such as fruit and vegetable wastes, animal manure and/or seaweed.

A bulk quantity of sawdust is very useful but don't compost it all at once. Keep it in a heap, well watered, for at least a month. It can then be added to your compost a bit at a time. Sawdust can also be used as a mulch.

# Seawater

Despite its high salinity, sea water is very nutritious. It is constantly replenished with chemicals from coastal runoff and deep sea volcanism along fracture zones and so it contains a complete range of both major and minor elements needed for plant growth.

Some people add seawater to compost; say one part seawater to a hundred parts of rainwater. Asparagus, kale, New Zealand spinach, beetroot and silverbeet all originated on sea-sprayed shorelines. They may benefit from spraying in the same proportions as your compost.

The best way to utilise sea water chemistry is to use seaweed—raw, dried or as a liquid extract.

# Seaweed

Seaweed is the perfect compost additive as all the necessary nutrients are concentrated in it from seawater.

Figures cited above show seaweed is highly enriched in nutrients. Seaweed absorbs these elements as separate entities (ions), not as combinations (compounds). So sea salt (sodium chloride) is not concentrated or even present, in that form, in seaweeds. Therefore, seaweed is not harmful as an additive to soil or compost. From the figures below the high enrichment it contains can be appreciated.

Collect seaweed when it is as fresh as possible because it loses its nutrients rapidly, particularly nitrogen. No need to wash, just chop with a spade and spread as a mulch or add into compost. Alternatively, make a liquid tea. If you are using seaweed as your major nutrient and trace element source, add dolomite to the soil when applying compost to your garden beds as seaweed does not concentrate magnesium.

# Seaweed Extract

These concentrates, usually of bull kelp, are excellent. The commercial products seem expensive but they go a long way: 10 ml diluted in 1 litre of rainwater acts as a foliage spray for fruit trees and makes a highly nutritious additive to a household compost bin. A dried meal from seaweed is also available commercially.

# Sheep Manure

Sheep, like cows, are ruminants, but the manure differs considerably. Sheep manure is dropped as pellets and is dehydrated. It is a concentrated product with a relatively high potassium content. Various biochemical compounds are also concentrated, including amino acids and enzymes.

These compounds increase the aroma of fruit and flowers and the oil content of herbs. When sheep are grazed on mint the oil content of the mint is increased. Intriguing, as we eat roast lamb with mint sauce or jelly.

Sheep manure is an accumulating problem under a shearing shed. To the gardener who can collect the manure it is a great gift. Spread generously over established beds or on spoiled hay for immediate planting or sowing of seed.

Outstanding results can be obtained from sheep manure. Most striking are sweet peas with bright, strong colours, good perfume and thick flower stalks up to 30 cm long. This reflects the potassium content, since potassium reinforces stalk and stem fibres and enhances flowering. Sheep manure also strengthens root development.

Sheep manure enriches compost, but add it at the end of the composting process, with dolomite and/or wood ash.

# Shellfish

Shellfish are a diverse group of marine animals whose soft parts are edible and whose hard parts, their shells, are rich in plant foods. Prawn, lobster and crayfish shells are composed of chitin, as are our fingernails, and bonded together with nitrogen, phosphorus and calcium. Bury them deep in your working compost heap and soon they and their smells will dissolve into plant food.

Oyster and mussel shells are basically calcium carbonate, with varying amounts of nitrogen, phosphorus, potassium and trace elements. Mussel shells disintegrate quicker than do oyster shells, which should be broken up before being added to compost.

# Shredders and Munchers

The small, electric-powered 'munchers' will reduce kitchen and garden wastes to piles of finely chopped material that will compost more rapidly than bulk waste. Shredders are larger, petrol-driven machines. They take thicker material, are faster and more robust. A good rotary lawn mower can chop up compost materials that are not too soggy.

In small gardens no machinery is needed. Most materials can be chopped with a sharpened garden spade.

# Slaters

Slaters are land-living relatives of crabs and lobsters. Also known as wood lice or pill bugs, they are unjustly labelled as pests since they do no harm to plants. Their part in the decomposition of vegetable matter is in working over yeasts and fungi. If they are browsing over your compost the moisture content will be just right.

# Slugs and Snails

Although much loathed for their destructive work in the garden, slugs and snails do have a function in the composting process.

Their rows of teeth, called radulae, and their mucous membranes digest cellulose, including newspaper and cardboard.

The leopard slug, which is much larger than the usual garden slug and easily recognisable, is of particular help in a heap of well wilted material. It eats only dead vegetation and plant products such as paper.

Some breeds of ducks eat slugs and snails, ferreting them out with great gusto.

If you have to kill snails, their shells add calcium and other minerals to the heap.

# Stinging nettles

Stinging nettles contain iron for green leaf production and are high in nitrogen. Add leaves to the compost as an accelerator or make liquid manure for green leaf plantings.

# Straw

Straw is the stubble of stalks and stems left after harvest. It is used as a mulch and compost filler or as chicken or stable litter. Barley, maize, oats, wheat, pea and other grain stubbles are cut for straw. Nutrient content of straw is low as most of the plant protein has been harvested, whilst the whole plant is cut as hay.

# Strip Trenching

This system of rejuvenating established garden beds makes compost and manure go a long way. With a narrow hoe make trenches 10 cm wide and deep with a 10-cm space between rows. In the first and third trench place fresh or mature manure; in the second trench, compost. Sow seed or transplant seedlings into the compost trench and compact the soil well. As the plants develop, their roots will benefit from the trenches of manure. The next crop is planted into the manured trenches. Worms will be very active in these trenches.

# Sulphur (S)

Sulphur is present in all plant materials and in all but very sandy soils. Decomposing in a covered compost heap, it becomes concentrated by sulphur-forming bacteria. Disturb the heap and smell the rotten egg gas— hydrogen sulphide.

With aeration, in warmed soil or compost, free sulphur or sulphides will oxidise and combine with other elements. They form sulphate salts of iron, potassium, calcium, magnesium and so on. These sulphates are soluble in water so the plants can absorb them. The sulphides, such as the mineral pyrite (iron sulphide), are insoluble in water. No matter how much pyrite is available, plants cannot absorb it.

Sulphur is important within proteins, enzymes and vitamins. Composts that have digested kitchen and garden wastes will have the correct balance of sulphur. Leaves of the cabbage family are particularly rich in sulphur—think of the smell of boiling cabbage.

Soils are seldom deficient in sulphur but in industrial areas it can be a pollutant, inhibiting plant growth. The denuded vegetation around Queenstown, Tasmania, shows the devastation caused by the emissions of sulphuric gases in the primary processing of sulphide mineral ores. Acid rain in North America and Europe is caused by sulphur emitted as an industrial waste product into the air.

# Superphosphate

Superphosphate and triple superphosphate are manufactured by treating phosphate rock with sulphuric acid. Phosphoric acid, a more soluble form of phosphate, is released.

Super has an abundance of sulphur which causes a microbiological imbalance in the soil. The production of humus in the soil is therefore reduced and acidity increased. All that Super leaves in the soil is a residue of harmful salts which discourages earth-worms.

When the microbiological life around them in the soil is not destroyed, earthworms concentrate organic phosphate. So, not only does Super impair the quality of your soil ultimately but it also inhibits the natural processes for concentrating phosphate. Further, the manufacture of superphosphate and the synthetic nitrogenous fertilisers are high energy- consuming industries.

# Tea Leaves

Empty the teapot into compost or mulch. It has a high nitrogen content and also contains phosphorus and potash.

# Temperature

Compost needs cooking. The graphs on page 41 shows changes in temperature during the cooking process in both covered heaps and tumblers. Increased temperatures are generated by anaerobic bacteria when air is excluded. By tossing or turning, aeration occurs and temperature drops, building up again as air is excluded. A gradual cooling is apparent until it reaches a constant temperature that approximates that of the air outside. You can feel the temperature fluctuations by thrusting your hand deep into the compost. You won't keep it there for long if the temperature is above 60°C. The high temperatures to help purify the finished product by cooking weed seed eggs and larvae of insects and nematode worms, as well as chemically changing organic toxins into harmless substances.

If you want to be more precise or set a project for high school students, use a thermometer rather than your hand. We use a preserving thermometer, having ruined two normal air thermometers in heated compost. If you want to demonstrate the power of a hot compost heap, wrap a raw egg in foil and place it in the middle of the heap. Come back in a couple of hours to a hard-baked egg!

# Trace Elements

In minute quantities these elements are essential in many plant functions. Chlorine, iron, manganese, zinc, molybdenum, copper and boron are micro-nutrients, often acting as catalysts rather than being part of a complex molecule. Deficiencies are reflected in plant growth abnormalities: whip tail in cauliflower is caused by molybdenum deficiency, yellow citrus leaves lack iron.

A trace element that is present in the soil in larger amounts than is required is a pollutant. High concentrations of any trace element will be toxic to some plants. Each species of plant has its own requirements and tolerances. Compost, which includes a variety of materials such as legume hays, animal manures and/or seaweed, will contain a balanced mix of trace elements.

Dramatic changes of vegetation are a useful tool in mineral exploration. On aerial photographs or satellite imagery, where plant growth has been adversely affected in an area of country, a rich deposit of minerals such as copper may be found.

# Tumblers

We have had great success with our home-made tumbler. It is a quick and efficient way to make compost. Make sure you have a good carbon/nitrogen mixture (see The Carbon/Nitrogen Cone at the back of the book). Chop or shred the waste materials. Fill the tumbler to about three quarters capacity. If the mixture is too dry, add water. Rotate the tumbler once or twice a day. Compost should be ready in ten days.

# Urine

A valuable resource, both from humans and farm animals, urine has high nitrogen and potassium values. Human urine can be added directly to compost or applied as a slow release fertiliser by soaking sawdust or wood charcoal in urine. I refer to this product as 'Rocking-Horse Manure'! Bedding of straw or hay absorbs urine from farm animals so it is excellent for composting, particularly as urine accelerates decomposition.

# Water

Water is a vital component as it is the prime source of adding hydrogen and oxygen into the biochemical mix. The quality of the water is very important as it can effect the composition of the microbial assemblages as well as earthworm activity. Rainwater is preferred and this is yet another reason for installing a tank. Suburban tap water may have high chlorine content at times which can alter the pH. Bore water may have elevated salt content with pH ranging from highly acidic to extreme alkalinity, so it will need a chemical analysis. (See also SEA WATER).

# Weather

Warm or hot weather will help a fresh heap of material to begin the complex biochemical processes that create compost but hot or cold weather is not a very significant factor. If a collection of suitable ingredients is put together in a heap, the cooking and digesting will begin. In cold periods the process will be retarded but not stopped. A cover in cold weather helps the initial warming that is necessary. In wet weather it will protect the heap from too much rain.

# Weeds

A weed is a plant growing in the wrong place. Many of our garden weeds were brought to Australia as ornamental plants, as seed contaminating commercial seed, or even in mattresses and the padded collars worn by working horses.

Weeds from the garden can be composted—get them before they seed. The following must be treated separately: nut grass, onion weed, oxalis and Tradescantia, known as wandering jew or creeping gentile. Dig these up carefully with all their roots and corms, pack them into opaque plastic bags with a little water and seal tightly. Keep in a warm spot or some months, until they have rotted completely.

Hay, straw and free-range animal manures may contain a variety of weed seed that will germinate if not burnt up in the composting process. If manure is applied directly to beds, burying it or covering it with mulch will reduce the weed problem. Learn to identify weeds in their early growth when they are easy to remove. Stinging nettles often grow out of free-range manure;cherish them as a compost additive for their iron and calcium content.

# Windrow

Windrows are elongate loaf-shaped piles of plant material such as compost as detailed for Indore method. I usually run mine east-west to maximise solar energy.

# Wine

Residues and pressings from the wine-making process make good compostable material and are especially high in potassium.

# Wood Ash and Soot

Wood ash is a valuable source of potash ($K_2O$). When it is derived from eucalypt hardwoods it also contains useful amounts of phosphate and an array of trace elements. The soot from wood fires concentrates these nutrients in even greater amounts.

Fresh ash is very alkaline and can upset the pH balance of your compost, so add at maturation, as for lime and dolomite. The alkalinity could also burn young plant roots so when applying to seed beds, spread ash 10 cm from rows of seedlings.

Coal ash, especially from Victorian brown coal briquettes, is suspect and should not be used, due to high tar and sulphur content.

# Worms

The term is fairly meaningless as there are many worm-like creatures that are totally unrelated to each other. Those which inhabit soil and rotting vegetation include:

**The annelids**—the most important group, see Earthworms.

**The platyhelminthes**—flat, arrow-headed, slimy worms that travel by expanding and contracting like elastic. They live under rocks as well as in rotting vegetation. It is not unusual to find them on the edge of a compost heap and although they look and feel repulsive, they can be useful; their slime or mucous may play a part in decomposing vegetation.

**The nematodes**—round, thread-like worms, including eelworms. Many of these are harmful to plants, being parasitic within the plant roots. Soil nematodes can be controlled by mulching thickly with compost. This organic matter contains fungi which entrap and destroy nematodes: an example of simple biological control of pests by organic means.

# Yarrow

Yarrow belongs to a group of herbs of the genus Achillea—mythologically powerful in healing Achilles' heel but also biochemically powerful in compost. Yarrow contains a complexity of organic compounds to stimulate microbiological activity and makes a potent liquid tea to accelerate compost activity.

# Yeasts

Yeasts are significant in the fermentation process of composting. Although present in rotting vegetation, particularly fruit, the process can be accelerated by adding brewer's or baker's yeast, bread scraps, vegemite, yoghurt or buttermilk.

# Yoghurt and Buttermilk

Yoghurt and buttermilk ferment readily and produce yeasts and other micro-organisms. Leftovers added to the compost heap will act as accelerators.

# Zinc (Zn)

Although present in plants in minute traces, zinc is an essential component of several plant enzymes. These enzymes are involved in the formation of complex organic compounds and in the regulation of water.

Zinc can be deficient in leached sands and calcareous soils, such as in southeast South Australia. Adequate zinc is provided by seaweed, corn stalks and all animal manures.

# Uses and Values of Composting Materials

| COMPOSTING MATERIALS | Mulch/Filler | Accelerator | Additives | N | P | K | Ca | Mg | S | Cl | Fe | Mn | Zn | Cu | B | Mo |
|---|---|---|---|---|---|---|---|---|---|---|---|---|---|---|---|---|
| Banana stalks | | | | ○ | ■ | | | | | | | | | | | |
| Blood & bone | | ✓ | | ■ | ● | ● | + | + | | + | | | | | | |
| Bran | | ✓ | | ● | ● | ● | | | | | | | | | | |
| Cardboard | ✓ | | | | | | | | | | | | | | | |
| Carpet underfelt | ✓ | | | | | | | | | | | | | | | |
| Chicken manure – fresh * | | ✓ | | ● | ○ | | + | + | + | + | + | + | | + | + | |
| Clever Clover | | ✓ | | ● | ○ | ● | + | + | + | + | + | + | + | + | + | |
| Comfrey | ✓ | ✓ | ✓ | ● | ● | ● | + | + | | + | | | + | | | |
| Cow manure – fresh * | | ✓ | ✓ | ● | ○ | ○ | + | + | + | + | + | + | + | + | + | |
| Dandelions | | ✓ | ✓ | | ○ | | + | + | | ○ | | | + | | | |
| Dolomite | | | ✓ | | | ■ | ■ | + | | | | | | | | ? |
| Duck manure – fresh * | | ✓ | ✓ | ● | ○ | + | + | + | + | + | + | + | | + | | |
| Earthworm cast | ✓ | ✓ | ✓ | ● | ● | + | + | + | + | + | ? | ? | ? | ? | ? | |
| Egg shells | ✓ | ✓ | ✓ | ● | + | ● | + | + | | + | | | | | | |
| Feathers | | | | ■ | | | | | | | | | | | | |
| Fish meal | ✓ | | | □ | ● | ● | + | + | + | + | + | + | + | + | + | |
| Fungi | ✓ | ✓ | | ■ | | | | | | | | | | | | |
| Goat manure | ✓ | ✓ | | ● | ○ | + | + | + | + | + | + | + | | | + | |
| Grass clippings | ✓ | ✓ | | ● | + | + | + | + | + | + | + | | | | | |
| Green manure – legumes | ✓ | ✓ | | ■ | ● | + | + | + | + | + | + | | | + | | |
| – non-legumes | ✓ | | | ○ | ○ | ● | + | + | | ○ | | | | | | |
| Guano – bat | | | | ■ | ● | + | + | + | | | | + | | | | |
| Hair | | | | ■ | | | | | | | | | | | | |
| Hay – legume | ✓ | ✓ | | ○ | ● | ● | + | + | | + | | | | + | | |
| – non-legume | ✓ | | | + | ○ | ○ | ○ | | | | | | | | | |
| Horse & Elephant manure * | ✓ | | | ○ | ○ | ○ | | | | | | | | | | |

The symbols used are:

- ✓ Important
- ■ more than 10%
- □ 5 – 10%
- ● 1 – 5%
- ○ 0 – 1%
- + trace
- ? possible trace

elemental content as percentage of dry matter.

\* Dried manure contains less nitrogen and micro-organism activity

Materials listed:

- Leaves
- Limestone
- Micro-organisms – aerobic
- – anaerobic
- Molasses
- Paper
- Phosphate rock
- Pigeon manure – fresh *
- Pig manure – fresh *
- Prawn shells
- Rabbit manure *
- Rock flour – granitic and basaltic
- Sawdust
- Sea water
- Sea weed – fresh *
- – meal
- – liquid extract
- Self mulching legumes
- N.Z. Spinach
- Sheep manure – fresh *
- Slugs & Snails – living
- – shells
- Stinging nettles
- Wastes – Citrus
- – Coffee
- – Garden
- – Kitchen
- – Wine pressings
- Wood ash (*Eucalyptus*)
- Yarrow
- Yeasts and Yoghurt

# Bibliography

Darwin, Charles, 1945, *Darwin on Humus and the Earthworm*.Faber & Faber, London. First published 1881 as *The Formation of Vegetable Mould through the Action of Worms with observations on their habits*. John Murray, London.

Dean, Esther, 1977, *Esther Deans' Gardening Book; Growing without Digging*. Harpercollins, Sydney.

Edwards, Clive, A. (Editor), 1998, *Earthworm Ecology*. Soil & Conservation Society, Iowa – St. Lucie Press Boca Racon Florida.

Grieve, Mrs. M., 1982. *A Modern Herbal*, Dover Publ. New York. First published 1931 by Harcourt, Brace & co., New York with the sub-title The Medicinal, Culinary, Cosmetic and Economic Properties, Cultivation and Folk-lore of Herbs, Grasses, Fungi, Shrubs and Trees with all their modern scientific uses.

Heath, Jim, 1989. *The fly in your eye*. J & E Publishing, Perth.

Howard, Sir Albert, 1945. *Introduction to Darwin on Humus and the Earthworm*. (see Darwin, 1945)

Howard, Sir Albert, 1947. *An Agricultural Testament*. Oxford University Press, London.

Kipling, Rudyard, 1940. *The Definite Edition of Rudyard Kipling Verse*. Hodder & Stoughton, London

LOVELOCK, James, 2009. *The Vanishing Face of Gaia: A Final Warning*. Allen Lane, Melbourne.

Roberts, M, 2009. *Starting out with Herbs*. New Holland Publishers, Sydney.

Storl, Wolf D, 1979. *Culture and Horticulture:- A philosophy of gardening*. Biodynamic Literature, Rhode Island, USA.

Taylor, David & Yvonne, 1993, *The Compost Book*, Reed Books, Sydney. Reprinted 1997, by Reed New Holland, Sydney.

# ACKNOWLEDGEMENTS

Despite all the encouragement, it was nigh impossible for this old dog to learn new tricks! So I sincerely appreciate the efforts and patience of Virginia Conroy who sorted me and my laptop out. Virginia also handled the e-mail traffic. Viginia's husband Phil Conroy freely discussed his 'hands-in' knowledge of worm farming and gave me a stack of relevant literature.

My gardening friends made suggestions regarding the content of this book; particularly after reading the first draft. My gratitude goes out to Rob Allsop. Rob and I have been gardening together for 25 years and I feel that our mutual understanding is expressed in Rob's illustrations.

# NOTES

# NOTES

Frst published in Australia in 2010 by

New Holland Publishers (Australia) Pty Ltd

Sydney • Auckland • London • Cape Town

www.newholland.com.au

1/66 Gibbes Street Chatswood NSW 2067 Australia

218 Lake Road Northcote Auckland New Zealand

86 Edgware Road London W2 2EA United Kingdom

80 McKenzie Street Cape Town 8001 South Africa

Copyright © 2010 in text: David Taylor

Copyright © 2010 in illustrations: Rob Allsop

Copyright © 2010 New Holland Publishers (Australia) Pty Ltd

A record of this publication is held at the National Library of Australia

ISBN 97817477069741.


Publisher: Diane Jardine

Production Manager: Olga Dementiev

Publishing Manager: Lliane Clarke

Project Editor: Rochelle Fernandez

Designer: Amanda Tarlau

Printer: Ligare Book Printers, Sydney, New South Wales


10 9 8 7 6 5 4 3 2 1